THE SEVENTH YEAR STRETCH

NEW YORK METS: 1977-1983

THE SEVENTH YEAR STRETCH

NEW YORK METS: 1977-1983

BY GREG PRATO

Written by Greg Prato
Printed and distributed by Greg Prato Writer, Corp.
Published by Greg Prato Writer, Corp.
Front cover design by Greg Prato
Baseball cards on the cover used with permission by Panini America, Inc.
First Edition, September 2015

ISBN: 9781516895281

INTRODUCTION

Why a book about one of the Mets' darkest eras in their entire history, when they didn't even post a single winning season over a seven-year span? A valid question, dear friend. But please, let me explain. First off, while the Mets posted an unpleasant record of 434 wins and 641 losses from 1977-1983, it was during these years that they started "putting the pieces together" that would eventually lead to their successful run between 1984-1990, when they would go 666-466, and of course, win the 1986 World Series.

Secondly, it wasn't that the Mets didn't possess talent on their roster. For much of this span, a future Hall of Fame manager oversaw the club (Joe Torre) with the help of two all-time greats as coaches (Willie Mays and Bob Gibson), the 1978 NL ERA champ was one of their leading pitchers (Craig Swan), former and future NL Cy Young Award Winners were spotted on the mound (Randy Jones and Mike Scott, respectively), one of the era's great relief pitchers - who for a spell, was the all-time MLB save leader - originally came up with the Mets (Jeff Reardon), not to mention the 1976 NL Rookie of the Year co-winner (Pat Zachry), a slugger who led the NL in home runs in 1979 and 1982 (Dave Kingman), another slugger who was the 1977 NL MVP and 5x All-Star (George Foster), the 1980 NL Gold Glove winner for second base (Doug Flynn), a 4x All-Star catcher behind the plate (John Stearns), and a talented player that also attracted the attention of many young ladies (Lee Mazzilli).

And thirdly, well, let me tell you a bit about how I became a Mets fan. The first Mets game I ever attended was in 1979, I believe, when my grandfather (a diehard Mets fan) took two of my cousins and myself to a day game at

Shea. Since I was only seven years old at the time and didn't know diddly about the sport yet, my only vivid memory is visiting the men's restroom at one point, and spotting a toilet overflowing. But by late '81, I found myself finally following pro sports. And one of the first teams I rooted for was…the New York Yankees. And this made sense, as my father seemed to enjoy the Bronx Bombers at the time, and they appeared to be on the path to winning another World Series, before they experienced some difficulties against Fernando and the Dodgers.

The following year, three events occurred that ended my brief affiliation with the Yanks as my top team - they let my favorite player at the time walk away (Reggie Jackson), they got off to a sluggish start, and the final straw was when they lost the 1982 "Mayor's Trophy Game" to the Mets. That, was how I became a Mets fan. Honestly, if I knew my baseball history and was aware that the "Mayor's Trophy Game" was meaningless, how many championships the Yanks had won compared to the Mets (we were still quite a way from the dawn of the Internet, where this sort of info was just a click or two away), or if I had a crystal ball and saw how the Mets would often torment/torture their fans after the 1980's, I very well may have stood firm with my original baseball choice. But I have indeed remained loyal ever since - for better or for worse.

So it was the 1982 season that I began following the Mets. Watching as many games as possible on television, it seemed like the Mets were on the right track for the first half…until they endured a horrific 15-game losing streak in August, which totally sunk their season. In fact, I remember saying to myself, "If the Mets lose one more game, I'm no longer a fan." And they proceeded to lose another one…and another one…and another one…*and I remained a fan.* I then attended my second-ever Mets game with my father and two neighbors late in the season - which was on "Fan Appreciation Day" (I can't recall the exact date nor what team they were playing). I do remember an obscure pitcher by the name of Carlos Diaz signing my Mets Yearbook before the game, and watching Dave Kingman warm up by playing catch nearby, and yours truly shouting out his name repeatedly, until he finally offered some acknowledgement by uttering, "WHAT?!" Me asking, "Can you please sign my yearbook?" And him replying, *"Nah,"* and continuing his pre-game preparation.

Up next, was the national anthem. Only one problem, I realized I did not have my ticket in my pocket (my father was holding it for me), and since I was not familiar with Shea, I had no idea where the heck my seat was located. After wandering around for a while, I finally saw my dad (who was angrily yelling my name and waving), and I took in the game, which I remember the Mets winning. But the excitement wasn't completely over - I left Shea with a free blue and orange Mets winter hat (with I believe either a Maxwell House or Folgers logo sewn on the back), and when a bus driver with poor driving skills was creating traffic coming out of Shea, my father rolled down his car window to tell the gentleman, "If you had a brain, you'd be dangerous!" before speeding off.

So while the Mets from this era may not have been the most successful in the win column, they were still full of characters and provided many memorable moments - quite a few of which still remain in my standout memories of childhood. And the way I came to doing a book about this forgotten era of Mets history is the same way I've come to do all my previous books - it was a subject I was interested in reading about, but there was no book on the marketplace that focused solely on it. Now, there is finally a book that fills in all the blanks from the dawn of the "Midnight Massacre" to when a surprise trade brought one of baseball's superstars to the Mets, and promptly helped turn the franchise around.

Let's go Mets!
Greg Prato

p.s. Questions? Comments? Feel free to email me at gregprato@yahoo.com. And also, thank you to Rachel Levitsky at MLBPAA for all the help setting up interviews!

CAST OF CHARACTERS

Gary "Baba Booey" Dell'Abate - Longtime Mets fan, 'The Howard Stern Show' producer, book author
Pete Falcone - Mets pitcher from 1979-1982
Mike Fitzgerald - Mets catcher from 1983-1984
Brent Gaff - Mets pitcher from 1982-1984
Tom Gorman - Mets pitcher from 1982-1985
Steve Henderson - Mets left fielder from 1977-1980
Stephen Jacobson - Newsday reporter from 1960-2003, book author
Randy Jones - Mets pitcher from 1981-1982
Jerry Koosman - Mets pitcher from 1967-1978
Skip Lockwood - Mets pitcher from 1975-1979
Tim McCarver - Mets TV broadcaster from 1983-1998
Dan Norman - Mets right fielder from 1977-1980
Rick Ownbey - Mets pitcher from 1982-1983
Charlie Puleo - Mets pitcher from 1981-1982
Lenny Randle - Mets third baseman/second baseman from 1977-1978
Jeff Reardon - Mets pitcher from 1979-1981
John Stearns - Mets catcher from 1975-1984
Craig Swan - Mets pitcher from 1973-1984
Walt Terrell - Mets pitcher from 1982-1984
Mike Torrez - Mets pitcher from 1983-1984
Bobby Valentine - Mets third baseman/shortstop/second baseman/first baseman from 1977-1978, Mets coach from 1983-1985, Mets manager from 1996-2002
Steve Zabriskie - Mets TV broadcaster from 1983-1989
Pat Zachry - Mets pitcher from 1977-1982

CHAPTERS

This book is dedicated to my grandfather, Albert Conrad, who was first a loyal Brooklyn Dodgers fan, and then a loyal Mets fan - from their inception in 1962 until his passing in 1988.

CHAPTER 1:
A TRIP DOWN
METS MEMORY LANE
WITH BABA BOOEY

GARY "BABA BOOEY" DELL'ABATE [Longtime Mets fan, 'The Howard Stern Show' producer, book author]: My dad [Salvatore Dell'Abate] was a crazy, crazy Dodger fan. My dad grew up on the corner of Mott and Hester - right in the heart of Little Italy. And my dad tells the story of the Bobby Thomson home run [aka the "Shot Heard 'Round the World," which won the 1951 National League Pennant for the New York Giants over the Brooklyn Dodgers]. My dad was on the roof of his apartment building, listening on a transistor radio. And my dad told me this story for years - the part that I didn't get years later was my dad was also a very big gambler, so he must have had a lot of money on the game. And he said that when Thomson hit the home run, he threw the radio off the roof!

Years later, I did an appearance with Bobby Thomson at some autograph signing. I'm sitting next to him, and I told him the whole story, and he signed a picture which I gave to my dad, and when my dad died it's now sitting in the man-cave - it's a picture of Bobby Thomson and it says, "Dear Sal, Sorry about the Radio. Bobby Thomson." And during that time, I got to see Ralph Branca [the Brooklyn Dodgers pitcher who gave up the home run] a lot, because I live up in Connecticut, not far from Bobby Valentine, and Branca is his father-in-law. I would go to a lot of Bobby's charity events, and I would talk to Branca. I remember talking to Branca once, and I was talking about something or other, and he goes, "Yeah, those goddamned people were stealing the goddamned signs!" But he was generally a nice guy.

Probably around the '69 season [Dell'Abate became a Mets fan], because I was a really, really little kid, and that's when they started to get good...it might have even been the season before. I just have a vague recollection of my dad watching the games all the time, and always having a Rheingold in his hand. But I remember the championship season [in 1969, during only their eighth season as a franchise, the Mets would defeat the favored Baltimore Orioles, four games to one], I think I got really involved in watching baseball, because again, I would have been eight years old. So that's sort of my first memory.

Here's my recollection of how it first started - my dad was a really, really big Dodgers fan, so when the Mets came to town, he was a big Mets fan. So my recollection - even as a little kid - my dad would take us to the Old-Timers' Game every year. That was like our big family outing - usually without my mom. So it was me, my dad, and my two brothers. And we would go to the Mets Old-Timers' Game. The Mets didn't have any old-timers, so they were getting a lot of other ones. I remember Duke Snider being at one, and I could swear I remember Joe DiMaggio being at one. Because they would get a lot of old-timers from other teams, but they would also get the New Yorkers.

I would watch it every day [during the 1969 season] because my dad was so excited. To have a team go from as bad as they were to World Series champs in a single season, my dad was so excited because he was a big Dodgers fan, and even them winning a World Series took so much time. So this was on the fast track for him. But as a little kid, it sort of skews your reality, because you just think that, "Oh, my favorite team wins all the time." It was great though. I could literally go around the horn and tell you every player at every position. I remember loving Tom Seaver that year, I remember loving Bud Harrelson, Cleon Jones, and

Tommie Agee - they were all players that the fans really connected with and really loved.

I remember I was probably in third grade, and my teacher, Miss D'Amato, she was older. She was very tough and very stern - she didn't seem like a particularly fun lady. And I will never forget the day she wheeled the TV into the classroom at 1:00 or 2:00 in the afternoon, and she said, "We are going to watch the Met game today." I was like, "Holy crap! Miss D'Amato is way cooler than I thought!" And I remember the day that they won the World Series [Thursday, October 16, 1969, at Shea Stadium], the game started while we were at school. It was a day game, and I remember running off the bus to get home, to be able to see the end of it on TV. So maybe I got home at 3:30 or 3:40, I remember sitting home alone and watching it. And that's sort of a bummer, because now, when these games happen, it's very communal and everybody's there to share it. But people were at work and at school - you see those pictures of people standing in front of an appliance store and watching the game. But I remember being at my house alone and watching it, and going out, and all the kids in the neighborhood came out and we were happy.

It was really tough to take [the Mets losing the 1973 World Series to the Oakland A's in seven games], because you didn't think they would get there. They get there [with a regular season record of only 82-79], so you say, "OK, we're just happy that they get there." Up until that time, weren't they the team with the worst record that ever made it to the post-season? But they got there. Great. And then they play Cincinnati, and they beat them [three games to two in the NLCS, which included a now-famous brawl between the Reds' Pete Rose and the Mets' Bud Harrelson in Game 3]. In my basement, in my man-cave, there is a photograph of Pete Rose and Bud Harrelson. It is a black and white photograph signed by Pete Rose - they're both in mid-punch, Pete looks like he's winning, Bud's got his head tilted to the left, I can see the sign in the back that says

4 The Seventh Year Stretch

"Getty = More Gas," and it's signed, "Gary, He won the game, I won the fight. Pete Rose, Hit King." So now, they get to the World Series, they're going to play the big bad Oakland A's. And the thing that I really do remember is they were up three games to two. So you're like, "OK, all you've got to do is win one of the next two games. We can do this." It was heartbreaking [after the Mets dropped the last two games to the A's at Oakland Coliseum, to lose the Series].

CHAPTER 2:
MID '70s

STEVE JACOBSON [Newsday reporter from 1960-2003, book author]: I thought that team was basically condemned to mediocrity. The general impression I have is that the farm system wasn't turning out very much. They still had some pitching left - they had Jerry Koosman and Seaver around from the '69 team, but they didn't have a lot of other position players. [Former Mets general manager] Joe McDonald had a reputation - which someone said - "For being able to look at a seed and see a flower." Which is a very nice thing, but he didn't produce a whole lot.

JERRY KOOSMAN [Mets pitcher from 1967-1978]: Well, when you say "a few," how many are a few? [In response to the question, "In the mid '70s, did you feel the Mets were just a few players away from another '69 or '73 type season?"] If you've got some key players at the right positions, you can do a lot. Look at the Cubs in 1969 - they played basically with their same eight guys every day. With a few guys in the right position, and they "ham and egg it," a lot of good things can happen.

SKIP LOCKWOOD [Mets pitcher from 1975-1979]: [Jon Matlack and Koosman] were very different. Matlack had a great curveball and great control of the plate, and Kooz was kind of all over the place, but a real gamer. Koosman would go out there and grind out nine innings in the heat in Philadelphia in the middle of the summer. Koosman was an extraordinary guy - he was just a bulldog. Matlack I remember having great stuff - enormous control of the plate. Great with his pitch control and his pitch selection. With Seaver, Matlack, and Koosman out there, you knew you had a chance every day at getting a win.

JOHN STEARNS [Mets catcher from 1975-1984]: I was just a rookie then. I was learning. But '75/'76, we still had a lot of those guys still playing from the '69 team. Like Koosman, Matlack, Seaver were there, you had Wayne Garrett, Bud Harrelson, Félix Millán, Ed Kranepool, John Milner, Cleon Jones, and veterans like Del Unser. I'm sure the mindset was it was still the core of the team, but it was getting older.

CRAIG SWAN [Mets pitcher from 1973-1984]: I can't remember what our best season was - '75 or '76 [the Mets' record in '75 was 82-80, and in '76 was 86-76]. I think it was when Joe Frazier was the manager. 1976 was the best season I had with the Mets.

JERRY KOOSMAN: Well, the '76 season sticks out for me personally, because I won 21 games that year, and also, that spring, my father died, so it was quite a year for me. [Randy Jones of the San Diego Padres] won 22 games, and our ERA's are pretty close to the same [Jones' ERA was 2.74, and Koosman's ERA was 2.64]. I can't remember strikeouts, if we were about the same there, too [Jones threw 93 strikeouts, and Koosman threw 200 strikeouts]. But they were pitching him every three days, so therefore, he got a win up on me [Jones finished with a record of 22-14, compared to Koosman's 21-10].

RANDY JONES [Mets pitcher from 1981-1982]: Definitely [Jones was aware that the 1976 Cy Young Award was a battle between himself and Koosman]. I had the big first half of 1976, and Kooz had the big second half that year. He really pitched well down the stretch in the second half - unfortunately, it wasn't quite enough. Let me put it this way - my first half was better than his second half, that's about all I can say. [Laughs]

SKIP LOCKWOOD: The things that happened to me were psychological as well as physical [in the 1976 season, Lockwood finished tied with the Houston Astros' Ken Forsch for 2nd place with most saves in the National League, with 19 - behind the Cincinnati Reds' Rawly Eastwick, who finished with 26]. I think getting a chance to pitch and being relied on a big league level, day in and day out, getting a chance to go out to the mound in situations where you had to save. And it builds one after another. So if you're pitching a couple and you get a save, you're going to pitch in another one.

For me, it was a building year. I was trying to establish myself, and the way that you do it is to have the confidence that the guys in front of you want you to come in. Seaver became a good friend and he would say to me, "You're coming in today. If I get a lead in the seventh or eighth, you're coming in. So get your fat ass ready to go!" He was a good guy that way. He was very helpful. Tom was very influential and an important guy in my career - and for the Mets obviously, in the years that he played there.

TIM McCARVER [Mets TV broadcaster from 1983-1998]:   I don't know that we on the Phillies felt that way [that playing the Mets in the mid to late '70s was an "easy win"], because you know that any major league team is dangerous if they can field a club. All you have to do is go back to 1964 and we [the St. Louis Cardinals] played the Mets the last three games of the season, and they won the first two, and we won the pennant on the last day of the season. No team was more hapless than the Mets in those days, but they were a dangerous team. So, I never felt that way as a player - I never felt that way about *any* team.

SKIP LOCKWOOD: Every day you go to the ballpark, you're trying to win. So we always thought we had a chance to win. We had great players, All-Star players - Rusty Staub, Dave Kingman was on the team, Lee Mazzilli, Buddy Harrelson. We had extraordinary talent on those teams those years. I thought we had a chance when we left spring training. But things didn't come together. The Reds had a powerful team if you remember at that point in time [that won the World Series back-to-back, in 1975 and 1976]. So it was hard to overcome, with Philly and Cincinnati. But I always thought we had a good team. We had great pitching - it was just a question of whether or not we could score enough runs.

CHAPTER 3:
1977 &
THE MIDNIGHT MASSACRE

SKIP LOCKWOOD: Well, you never do [know how a season will turn out]. Spring training is a chance to build a team. The team coalesces, comes together as you build momentum during the season. You don't win or lose seasons coming out of spring training. Hopefully, you trade for the kind of players you need. I thought that the team had a great opportunity when we left spring training that year.

CRAIG SWAN: At spring training, we definitely want to compete, and we thought we might - but still, we were losing players and the players we were getting were like, back-up players. They were either at the end of their career or mediocre at best, themselves. So you could kind of tell. By the end of April, we knew we were in trouble in '77. [Laughs] As a player, all I could do was really focus on my performance, and not really worry about the teams. I think playing on those teams that didn't score a lot of runs, in a way, it made me a better pitcher, because I knew I couldn't give up many runs and have a chance. It kind of made me buckle down and maybe try harder. But I think trying harder was actually the main reason I hurt myself so much - over-trying.

JOHN STEARNS: Joe Torre was a great person, first of all. And he showed up as a player for the Mets in '75. He was our third baseman. He just took me under his wing - I went to dinner with him a lot and hung out with him. He was showing me the ropes. I lived in Manhattan and he was in Manhattan a lot. On the road, he would take me to some of his places. He was our "veteran guy" - really a great guy. He played a couple of years, in then in '77 [on May 30th], they made him the manager. He was a natural as a manager - he knew what he was doing and he had a really calm, level personality. He didn't get too high or too low. Perfect. Obviously, a Hall of Fame type of manager. Just had a smooth set of emotions. You can't get too high on a good day and too low on a bad day, because you've got to come back tomorrow and do it again. He had that kind of demeanor that he was the same every day, and he carried that through into his managing career. A Hall of Fame manager and player - he was a great player, too. Just a great guy, helped me out a lot.

I remember when they named him manager, I was happy about it. I was the #1 catcher when that happened and I played about five years for him, and I was the #1 guy. I thought we got along well, even though my personality was much more volatile than his. I was more of a, "Let's just kick these guys' butts." I just wanted to play with...not anger, but I wanted to play hard and just wanted to win. And I didn't like the opponent. I think Joe was more of a smooth, easygoing type of approach to the game. And it worked for him - he could come out and play that way. Me? I wanted it to be 150% all the time, on "full speed ahead." That's just the style of game I played. Even though Joe and I had contrasting personalities, I thought we got along well. I certainly enjoyed playing for him - I thought he was an excellent manager.

JERRY KOOSMAN: Joe and I were good friends as teammates, and he then became manager, and as much as you know about the game, you still have a little learning curve there as a manger. So I'm sure he'll tell you that he probably would have done some things different. But he didn't have a whole lot to work with, either.

CRAIG SWAN: Joe moved from the locker room into the

front office there, but he was always kind of a "player's manager." Wasn't he a player/manager for that one year? [Torre was a player/manager for a short while in 1977, before retiring as a player on June 15th, to make room on the roster for the recently acquired Joel Youngblood] He couldn't do much. He was a nice guy and I liked Joe a lot - having played with him for a couple years there, it was different. You usually don't play with your manager. But he wasn't a screamer or yeller or anything like that. He was just doing the best he could with the talent that he had - which wasn't much.

JERRY KOOSMAN: We started trading some of our main players away. And our team was getting weaker and weaker. So, we went into those '77 and '78 years with gosh, you might say a Double A ballclub, on average. We just had no strength defensively, and certainly, offensively.

STEVE JACOBSON: [Writer] Dick Young was very harsh on Seaver at that time, and Young was an intimidating newspaperman - more than I had ever seen in New York. And he was in Donald Grant's ear. I remember writing a column shortly before that, about Grant's penny pinching and failure to recruit, and he said he had a marvelous team and he was proud that it was affordable. It *wasn't* a marvelous team…but it was affordable. And I argued with him as much as you could, "What good is a bad movie that's cheap? Who wants to go to it?" And that's what they had. There was a lot of penny pinching and the older I got, the more I realized that ownership is the most important thing they have - you can put any field manager on there and if ownership doesn't want to win and doesn't want to pay the price to win, it won't win. Unless they get very lucky…which they got in the first place, when they got Seaver - the lottery that the Mets reluctantly bid on with anticipation that they wouldn't get him.

JOHN STEARNS: We were in Houston in June. Seaver pitched one last game in Houston - I think he won that game [on June 12th, the Mets beat the Astros 3-1]. The next thing I know, he got traded and was gone right away. He was traded to Cincinnati, and was gone. And so that was it. I don't know if we even talked. Didn't really know who we got in that deal until they showed up. We got some young prospects for Seaver [pitcher Pat Zachry, second baseman Doug Flynn, left fielder Steve Henderson, and right fielder Dan Norman], but you never can get enough for a superstar like him.

SKIP LOCKWOOD: Oh, nobody saw the trade coming. I basically lost my ride to the ballpark. Tom and I went in together every day. He got me to buy a house out in Connecticut near him. He basically was gone in the middle of the night. I don't know exactly what the number was - I don't think he was asking for very much money. It was something there that Tom felt he wasn't being recognized by the team for his contribution, and I think it was something where he would not accept the fact that they wouldn't treat him as a superstar - which he was.

JERRY KOOSMAN: Two months before that, I wouldn't have expected it. But say, a week before, you might have expected it, because by then, there had started to get a little more publicity and animosity between Donald Grant and Tom, and Dick Young involved, writing those articles.

CRAIG SWAN: That was a tough one. Tom was a good friend by then. The way that happened, with Dick Young writing those articles - I don't really remember the articles, but I remember Tom being very upset by these articles. And we weren't too sure that M. Donald Grant wasn't behind that. Dick Young - prior to the free agency of 1976 - he was always on the players' side in his articles. And as soon as we got free agency, he switched right over to the owners' side -

which we thought was interesting and kind of strange. So, I don't know. M. Donald Grant kind of had him in his back pocket - we think - and caused the problems that eventually got Tom off the team. It was upsetting - he was the face of the franchise.

Another thing I forgot is that one of the reasons that I think they traded him was one of the reasons they traded a lot of the guys that were our representatives during the free agency and the strikes. And Tom was our representative for the team. So Tom would hold meetings and inform us what Marvin Miller and Dick Moss had told him. So a lot of those player reps, they got traded soon after free agency, because the owners didn't like them. They united us. So they were let go or usually traded.

STEVE JACOBSON: [Young] sold an awful lot of newspapers at the Daily News and at the Post, when he transferred. Dick didn't like free agency and players moving, but he moved from the Daily News to the Post as a "free agent" himself. And he could reach people in baseball management that other people couldn't. He had them spooked and they returned his phone calls and they didn't like him writing harshly about them, and he did that.

The Daily News was the largest circulating newspaper in the country at the time, and I don't believe before or since - I don't go back to Damon Runyon, and they weren't writing that kind of stuff - ever seeing people intimidated by a writer. And as another writer on a different paper, Young could fight for "print rights," where baseball management wanted the television cameras in first in the World Series, Young told them that was bullshit - that the writers who gave the team a million dollars worth of publicity all year should not be forced to take second place to TV. And on occasion, when the television cameras were - he thought - intruding, he would use a kind of language that forced the television camera people to edit their film.

JOHN STEARNS: Dick had an attitude. I don't know why he had an attitude. I got up there, and he was older - he had been around a while. But he had an attitude. And by that, I mean most writers come in and try to be friends with you and you can hold a conversation with them. I didn't see that from Dick. It seemed like he was mad. If you got off on the wrong foot one day with him, then he would storm off. I'm going, *"What's the matter with this guy?"* Wasn't he the official scorer, also? One time, he left something out on the scoring thing for me. I tried to talk to him about it, and he got all mad and defensive. He was a hard guy to like. That's Dick Young - he was hard to like.

STEVE JACOBSON: I had dinner with him any number of times, and in conversation. He was very abusive to some people, and he was not to me. I don't know why, but he just didn't.

JERRY KOOSMAN: I don't know how to measure it, but I'd certainly say [Young's feud with Seaver] had something to do with it, if not, lit the fuse.

CRAIG SWAN: [M. Donald Grant] was the president of the club. He was hired by Joan Payson, who owned the club [from 1961 through her death, in 1975]. He wasn't a real nice guy. I remember he called me into his office at Shea Stadium, and I was coming close to signing a contract...a real big one, like, *$35,000 a year.* [Laughs] He called me up in his office and I had no idea why I was up there. I got up there and said, "Why am I up here?" And he said, "Well, I just wanted to talk to you." I said, "This is a little scary for me." And he said, "That's what I'm trying to do." And I walked out. A lot of intimidation stuff. You could either buy into it or walk out. I just walked out.

He wasn't very well liked by the team. He wasn't really a "baseball guy." That's why we lost Whitey [Herzog]. Because when I first signed, Whitey was the minor league director - he decided where all the players were going to play and what class, and also, an instructor. One of the best baseball people that I had ever been around - besides maybe Bobby Winkles, who was my coach at Arizona State. That's what I heard - that him and M. Donald got in an argument and he walked, and went to St. Louis, and built that dynasty for years. We really lost a jewel there when we lost him.

STEVE JACOBSON: [Grant] was a patrician who was an older man and he managed Mrs. Payson's investments, and she was a Giant fan who objected and voted her stock against the Giants moving to California. And Grant was her "man on the team." Grant was a party entertainer - he could entertain or imitate a train or tell a joke. And sometimes, it was an off-color joke, and entirely inappropriate in public.

JERRY KOOSMAN: I think he ended up having too much to say. After Gil Hodges died [on April 2, 1972, at the age of 47, from a heart attack], the front office slowly started going downhill. You could tell it was going downhill, by some of the trades that were made. So I guess rather than build the club up and keep it strong, there were just some bad trades, bad moves being made. And pretty soon, we were depleted of our top talent.

SKIP LOCKWOOD: I had very little contact with people in the front office. It was interesting, when I got there, I was coming from the minor leagues - I was in Tucson, Arizona. So I was just happy to get back to the big leagues again, and coming back as a relief pitcher was way different than coming back as a starting pitcher. So I pitched a year and pitched well, and Tom said to me, "You need a long-term contract. At least a three-year deal. I'll see if I can get you something." So I guess he was the one that actually made the phone call to M. Donald, that got a three-year deal for me. When I went in, the numbers were the numbers, and I wasn't in any shape to negotiate for that. What Tom did and how he was treated by M. Donald Grant, I don't know. I never had much dealing with him myself. I don't think there was any love lost - especially after the winter meetings and the Cy Young Award presentation at the winter meetings. I think Tom wanted to be recognized and there was something there that Tom didn't like.

LENNY RANDLE [Mets third baseman/second baseman from 1977-1978]: It was getting a little strange, because some guys wanted to leave, and I couldn't figure out why. Because I'm a new kid on the block, and I'm figuring, "I love it here." I didn't go in the front office a lot - I stayed in the dugout and clubhouse. So whatever was going on between agents and management - M. Donald Grant was having some issues. Fans and people in the press were calling him names and all that, I was going, "Well, he has some social issues. I don't - I'm just going to hit the ball and go to my next team, because I know I'm not going to be here forever."

JOHN STEARNS: When I got over there, he was still the [board chairman]. I was really young, and I didn't really see much of him. I just got the feeling that he really didn't know much about baseball. I guess they put him in charge of running the club. The Payson family did that. I don't know how much he relied on...if he had scouts or the general manager or what, I don't know what he was doing. But he was not really a baseball guy, and made some decisions I think based on emotion. I didn't really like the Seaver trade, and that was the big trade there. I didn't understand why they would do that.

GARY "BABA BOOEY" DELL'ABATE: The thing I remember about the mid '70s Mets the most - that was the heartbreaker - was that they traded Tom Seaver. That was just *brutal.* Because for me, as a kid, he was hands down my favorite player. To the point where I remember they would go to shots in the stands of [Seaver's wife] Nancy, and I have a vague recollection they had a daughter that seemed to be about my age. I even knew all that about him. And I had all the yearbooks. He really was my favorite, favorite player. The thing that you have to understand - this is all pre-insane free agency and what's going on now. So players didn't leave teams the way...generally, it would be a blockbuster trade - which it sort of was. Well, it was a blockbuster for Cincinnati, it wasn't one for us! But I remember it being heartbreaking. For me, it was like, "OK, the Mets have clearly given up on being any good, because they're giving away their best player."

JOHN STEARNS: If you trade Tom Seaver, you've got to get some guys...I don't know if we got enough for Tom Seaver. At that time, we got four young players from the Cincinnati Reds. Of course, we didn't know how good they were, but I think Doug Flynn turned out to be the best player, and some of the other guys were OK. But you kind of want to get more than that for trading *Tom Seaver*. As far as all the other stuff running a team, I didn't know M. Donald Grant that well. But he didn't show his face much. I know he hired the general manager, Joe McDonald.

STEVE JACOBSON: I thought they got a lot of players who weren't going to play full-time. Doug Flynn was a nice fellow - who almost played basketball for Adolph Rupp in Kentucky - and Pat Zachry was also a charming fellow, who in the fit of anger, broke his toe by kicking a dugout step [in 1978]. You can't ask a pitcher who should be an occasional starter to be #1 or #2 on your staff. It doesn't happen. The promotion doesn't produce that kind of a result. Steve Henderson turned out to be a useful player, but just not enough. A player who could be your third outfielder, but don't expect him to be the star on your team.

GARY "BABA BOOEY" DELL'ABATE: I remember talking to my dad, and saying, "Who the hell is Pat Zachry? Really, who is that? Let me understand this, dad - we gave away the greatest pitcher in the history of the franchise, who took us to two World Series and won one of them...*for who?"*

PAT ZACHRY [Mets pitcher from 1977-1982]: Well, Rawly Eastwick apparently had some kind of a no-trade agreement in his contract, and he wouldn't go. And they said, "Well, OK" - so I happened to be the pitcher. That as my understanding.

JOHN STEARNS: Doug Flynn was a very solid person and player on the infield. He wasn't really an offensive type of player, but he was a great defensive player in the middle infield. He could play second or shortstop. He ended up being our second baseman for several years, and could really turn the double play. He won a Gold Glove [in 1980]. He was a good defensive second baseman.

Steve Henderson started out unbelievable in '77. When he first came over, for the second half of that season, he actually looked like a superstar for the two or three months that he played that year for us. I mean, he was just *drilling the ball.* He hit .297. He just tore it up for three months [and came in second that year in the NL Rookie of the Year voting, behind Andre Dawson]. The thing that was amazing about it was we really thought we had a #3 hole type of hitter in Steve Henderson coming out of that trade in '77. And I don't know what happened - he never showed us that again on a consistent basis. And then he was gone within a couple of years. We traded him.

Dan Norman was another big, strong kid that played for us. He was a Triple A type of prospect looking guy when he came over for the Seaver trade. He never really did step in and make the big league club. And then Pat Zachry was a pretty good pitcher. More of a #4 or #5 starter guy, but he did a pretty good job. I know he was in our starting rotation for three or four years. He wasn't bad - he just didn't have #1 or #2 type of stuff. But he had a real good changeup and slider, and he could throw his secondary pitches when he was behind in the count. Didn't throw real hard, but he was a decent pitcher.

PAT ZACHRY: Absolutely not [in response to being asked if he could see a trade coming]. I had no idea. I was the co-Rookie of the Year the year before [along with San Diego's Butch Metzger], and I thought I would die a Cincinnati Red. But apparently, not. It was a shock. To all of us, it was a shock. Actually, there was a couple of mixed emotions - the shock of being traded from the team you grew up with and since having done well the year before, that was another shock, and then having to go to a last place team was another shock. I think the greatest part of the whole thing - as far as myself - was the relation that I was able to develop with [pitching coach] Rube Walker and Joe Torre.

CRAIG SWAN: Zach was a pretty good pitcher. Unfortunately, he didn't have the Cincinnati Reds' bats like he had when he got over here. The Big Red Machine, they were real good in the '70s. And Dan Norman, he was just a marginal player, and Doug Flynn was a great second baseman - not much of a batter. Steve Henderson was a pretty good player. But I don't know - we weren't going to go anywhere with Tom anyway, because we didn't have the offense. I always wondered if he spent his whole career with the Mets, would he have won 300 games? [Seaver finished his career with 311 wins] Maybe not. Especially in the late '70s. He got out of there, and that was a good thing for him.

PAT ZACHRY: [Zachry's now wife] Sharron and I were supposed to be married, so what I had to do was explain it all to her, ask her to pack everything up...I've got to back up on this. She was at the time, a schoolteacher in Houston. And she had packed all of her things and had driven her little '70 Karmann Ghia convertible to Cincinnati with a friend, and I flew the friend home - we had planned the wedding and had made all the arrangements. All the notices had been sent out, we were receiving gifts, all these different things were supposed to take place. And then three days before, I got traded.

I walked out of the clubhouse that night and said, "Alright, I've got to go home and pack, because I've got to go to New York tomorrow" - instead of being in Cincinnati for another week, and getting this thing done. I said, "Honey, I'll be back. Would you take your car and get it shipped - try to get mine shipped to New York and yours to Texas." So she did all that. Flew back the next day, we went to a justice of the peace, the day after that, I flew back to New York again, met the team in...I believe we were headed to Chicago for I think it was a week-long road trip. And she had time to take care of all her stuff and got our things put together and driven to New York, and had everything packed up and shipped to New York.

There was never any doubt after that, that I had a keeper. We came in, made as many friends as we could, found a place to live. We got very, very lucky. We've been together 38 years - ever since. We had got the wedding done in Cincinnati, and that was all the "official" that we needed right there. And it's been 38 years - three children, we've got four grandchildren now, and everything's wonderful. It was a good way to start a marriage, I guess.

DAN NORMAN [Mets right fielder from 1977-1980]: They want you to come out with a bang. Henderson did - Steve came out and did real well. And Flynn was starting second base, and Zachry was in the starting rotation. So yeah, they were living up to the bill.

STEVE HENDERSON [Mets left fielder from 1977-1980]: We were a bunch of young kids. I think they were trying to rebuild a team. I don't want to necessarily say "rebuild," but they were adding some parts to help the team win. Like I said, they brought a lot of young guys over there - Zach was still young at the time, Flynn, myself, and Norman. And also, I think the following year, we wound up getting guys like Willie Montañez and Frank Taveras. It got a little interesting...until people started getting hurt.

DAN NORMAN: I think they did [get good players in return for Seaver].

STEVE HENDERSON: To be honest with you, I was just happy to be there. As far as the pressure part of if, I had good guys around me. Guys like Jerry Koosman, John Milner, and Lenny Randle - they took all the pressure off of me. And Joe Torre was great. He was a guy that took care of me pretty good over there. And I've got to make sure I say Stearns - without a doubt.

PAT ZACHRY: Oh gosh, yeah [veteran pitchers such as Koosman and Matlack were helpful to Zachry]. Just tried to make you fit in, help you with whatever they could. I was glad to see them both get a good break and get traded later, and go to good teams.

DAN NORMAN: They sent me to Triple A, and I think a few of the guys weren't too happy that I was traded there, because when they traded me to the Mets and went to Triple A, they released a popular outfielder, named Lee Iorg. So the players on the Triple A team weren't too happy that I was coming, because they released this guy. It took a little while for them to warm up to me. But when they saw how hard I was playing and the numbers I was putting up, they warmed up real quick.

STEVE HENDERSON: I really appreciated Jerry Koosman, because Jerry Koosman was a good friend of Tom Seaver's - probably still is - and he pulled me to the side, and said, "Don't be concerned about the pressure of Tom Seaver and everything. Just go out there and play ball." They treated me real well. Because they had been together a long time - they had won the '69 World Series and everything. I was appreciative for that.

DAN NORMAN: They were good teammates. They would give you some advice here and there. One guy that gave me some advice was John Milner. I think I was 21, maybe 22 when I got called up, and he didn't know me at all. He said, "This city can run you, or you can run the city. Make sure you get your rest." So, I took that to heart. That was the one thing that really stuck with me, and that came from John Milner. And then we ended up playing together again when the Expos.

STEVE HENDERSON: No [it didn't take Henderson long to adjust to New York], because I'm from Houston, Texas. Houston is just as big as New York. The only thing that took me a while was to make sure I got the right cab that would take me from the hotel to Shea Stadium. I got in a cab one time that took me all around the city, just to get me to Shea Stadium…and I was staying at a hotel right up the street! But I didn't know no better. I found out real quick.

PAT ZACHRY: Well, from a baseball standpoint, I went from first place to last place, and that was kind of difficult. But on the other hand, I got to play under Joe Torre, who I still think was one of the most influential people that I ever met, and I still think he's one of the best baseball people that were ever in the game. And played with a lot of really fine athletes and guys that were coming up and going down. Got to witness a lot of Hall of Fame careers, and the beginnings of some Hall of Fame careers.

STEVE HENDERSON: Whenever I see Mr. Seaver, I always tell him, "Thank you." That's all I can say on that. Because I got to the big leagues - I was in Triple A and I got to the big leagues.

GARY "BABA BOOEY" DELL'ABATE: It's one thing to get rid of your best player. But it's another thing to get rid of *the heart and soul* of your team. That really was the difference. I'm trying to think of an analogy...like, Patrick Ewing was with the Knicks, and he was certainly their star player. And he was liked, but I don't know that Patrick Ewing was loved. *Seaver was loved.* And there really was no explanation. I don't know what the Mets' explanation was. To the fans, it was like, "You just gave away our best player - the heart and soul of our team, Rookie of the Year, the 1969 season, the 1973 season...why?" I don't think they could ever really fully explain. They took a chance, and it was a really terrible chance.

CRAIG SWAN: I don't really remember that one too much [Dave Kingman was traded to the San Diego Padres for Paul Siebert and Bobby Valentine, on the same date as the Seaver trade]. Dave had already played for a number of teams. He got traded around. Dave was a great teammate, we loved water sports together, so we did a lot of stuff in spring training on jet bikes, boats, and fishing. A baseball player is kind of used to losing his friends, because they're always getting hurt and they're done, or they get traded or something. It's a strange profession that you build up pretty strong relationships, and they're gone the next day. So I do remember it, but it wasn't like Seaver getting traded.

BOBBY VALENTINE [Mets third baseman / shortstop / second baseman / first baseman from 1977-1978, Mets coach from 1983-1985, Mets manager from 1996-2002]: I thought it was a really friendly organization. Joe McDonald was a really nice guy, Joe Torre was a really nice guy, Joe Pignatano had played with my father-in-law [Ralph Branca], he was a really nice guy - he was a coach on the team. Rube Walker was a coach on the team and he had played with my father-in-law. So it was very welcoming for me.

STEVE JACOBSON: [The phrase "Grant's Tomb," which was used to describe Shea Stadium after the Seaver trade, due to poor attendance] first appeared on one of the banners. The banners were created by Met fans and by a sign-maker that had season tickets and would make placards expressing various things, like "RON SWOBODA IS STRONGER THAN DIRT" and "IS ED KRANEPOOL OVER THE HILL?" and "GRANT'S TOMB." Mets management tried to stop the banners and the placards, and it turned out to be a mistake that they recognized, and allowed it, and then they produced "banner day." And those banners were harsh on Grant at that time.

BOBBY VALENTINE: One of those years was the blackout [on July 13, 1977, which occurred during a game at Shea, when the Mets were playing the Cubs, with Lenny Randle batting and Ray Burris pitching]. I might have even been on deck - that was weird, I remember that.

LENNY RANDLE: When the lights went out, y'know, we wore the white pinstripes suits. Automatically, we saw each other in the dark. So the "clowns" or the fun guys of the club said, "Let's do an imaginary infield." I remember us being clowns on the field with no ball - we took the best infield, with no errors! [Laughs] We did an imaginary 'Laurel and Hardy' or 'Abbott and Costello' type "Who's on First?" But we took the greatest infield. I think Kranepool was the hitter, and Valentine, Doug Flynn, Stearns - with no ball. We took regular infield like it was a regular infield with lights...and the fans gave us a standing ovation! [Laughs] Because they could see the white dotted suits chasing an imaginary ball, and catching and throwing to first. So we were entertaining them, because some of them were getting nervous - some of the people were a little antsy.

Somebody yelled, *"Free ice cream at Baskin-Robbins!"* So there was a line for that - including the players - because it was all going to melt. And then somebody yelled, *"There's a lady stuck in the elevator!"* So we went to go help people stuck in the elevators. And we thought the game would continue. I don't know if we thought that Son of Sam turned the switch off [Son of Sam was still at large at that point, and wouldn't be apprehended until August 10th]. We figured it was just part-time - not permanent. So suddenly, we were back in the clubhouse, with candles and lighters and whatever, so we could see. I don't think anybody changed clothes - I think everybody went home in their uniforms. It was a crazy night. We thought God had said, "OK. We're going to take a time out and everybody reflect." [Laughs] There were all kinds of quotes - "Maybe this is a sign?" "What kind of sign are you thinking? You mean, 'end of the world' sign?" All kind of "imaginations" went on while the lights were out. Little did we know, the whole city, the lights went out [the entire city's power would return by the evening of July 14th].

JOHN STEARNS: We were sitting in the dugout, and Lenny Randle was hitting. The guy [Ray Burris] was throwing the ball, and the lights went out. I don't know what Lenny did - he must have dove on the ground, because I don't know if he lost sight of the pitch or not. It was really a shock - you're sitting there, playing a major league game, and the lights go *"bup"* just like that. We thought it was something that went out - the electricity - at the stadium. So we were sitting around there for a while. We didn't even go into the locker room for five or ten minutes. Then when I went in there, I thought we were going to play the game - I thought they were working on it. Sooner or later, it must have been a half an hour or 45 minutes later, they said that the game was off. No more lights anywhere. So we had no lights, the game was called, and we had no electricity for the subway, either.

There was a couple that had come to the game - newlyweds. They were staying in Manhattan, and I was walking out to my car, and they were standing in the parking lot, and didn't know how they were going to get down there. So I said, "Get in the car," and I took the couple who were on their honeymoon - because I lived in Manhattan that year, on the upper eastside - and I dropped them off at their hotel in Manhattan! [Laughs]

We were in a dark clubhouse - it was hard to shower, because they had emergency lighting going on, but the lights weren't really good in there. It was "old Shea Stadium" - it was a 1960's built stadium, which doesn't compare to the stadiums and the clubhouses of today. But it was OK, we weren't complaining - we were in the big leagues. Today, when you go into a major league clubhouse, you have a full kitchen of gourmet food, and the places are beautiful - they're large and beautiful locker rooms. It's not like you're playing sports, it's like you're out to a resort, somewhere. Back then, a locker room was *a locker room.* But we were in the locker room after the blackout. Finally, they called the game. I finally got showered up, walked out to my car, and I ran into the couple and I gave them a ride to Manhattan. Pretty amazing. The thing that I remember about it is Lenny hitting, and the lights going out as the guy was releasing the ball. And I'm going, "Oh my God!" If I was hitting, I would have dove back off the plate.

That night, I had to walk up to my apartment - it was dark. I had an apartment on about the second floor of a building on 77th and Second, and I walked up in darkness. I think I went to bed that night with no lights, but then they got it back on. It was definitely a shock. We had to finish the game later [on September 16th, with the Cubs winning by a score of 5-2.]. My first impression when it went out was that it was a "local thing," and they'd get it fixed over at the electric plant or wherever that comes from. And then after a while, you started to wonder, "What is going on?" And then they said the game was called, and that was it. Kind of a shocker, but one of those things where you've got to keep going. When you play a baseball game every day for six or seven months, - which includes spring training - you've got to get in a groove and just go. There was no time to do much thinking about it - we had a game the next day. It was kind of a shock and a unique experience.

LENNY RANDLE: Well, you call it "a massacre," I call it an opening of the world of baseball on the potentials of who can go where and when and why. It's like, you got your Ripkens, your McCoveys - some players just never get traded. The "franchises." And then you see Tom, you say, "Wow. If Tom is going, *we all can go.*" That's basically what everybody started saying. Jerry Grote started getting nervous, and guys go, "Well, I guess there's 30 other teams that might want us." It was kind of like a loose but serious moment, because no one felt like they were invincible. It was a weird situation.

CHAPTER 4:
1978 & 1979

SKIP LOCKWOOD: The years I spent in New York, the role as a closer at that point in time wasn't that well developed. And often was the case, you'd have to pitch two, three, or more innings to close a game. So it wasn't like you only came in for the ninth inning or the eighth and ninth inning. The role of closer was changing, and I was working with Bob Apodaca out of the bullpen, and we were trying - the two of us - to be the closer. So I didn't get all the chances for saves. It was Apodaca and I. But I got enough, so it wasn't like I got every chance - I got quite a few. And then Joe Torre took over as manager, and he liked the way that I went out there, so I got more and more chances to close the end of the game. So the whole time in New York I thought was a good time - a learning time. A chance for me to live close to a big city for a period of time. Those years were clearly the best of my career.

The pitching coach in those days tried to stay away from the pitchers that were pitching well, and help the pitchers that were pitching poorly. And I pitched there for four years, so Rube Walker [who served as the Mets' pitching coach from 1968-1981] and I were social and talked about a lot, but not so much helpful. The other players on the team were very helpful to me. But the pitching coach was there as a fundamental guy. He would help you with your motion, but the subtleties of pitching and how to get a little bit more bite on your curveball and stuff like that, we got between us - the pitchers helped themselves more than...not to take anything away from Rube. I thought Rube was a good pitching coach. But he knew enough to leave you alone if you were going good.

PAT ZACHRY: Rube was as nice a man as you'd ever want to meet. Not pushy at all. A little more unlike Larry Shepard [the Cincinnati Reds pitching coach from 1970-1978], because Larry was more of a professorial type than Rube was. Rube, having been an old catcher, just whatever you wanted to put down, he'd be happy to call it and let you throw it. "Throw it and he'd catch it" kind of guy Rube was. Very easy to work with and work for. A super man, a super nice fella.

JERRY KOOSMAN: My ERA was in the lower threes, I believe both years [Koosman's ERA in '77 was 3.49 and in '78 was 3.75, however, his records were 8-20 and 3-15], but I just wasn't getting any runs. I know in 1978, I got 26 runs scored for me *all year.* You're not going to win with that type of offense.

SKIP LOCKWOOD: It's rare that I think back and pat myself on the back [that Lockwood had success in '77 and '78 - 20 saves and 15 saves - on bad Mets teams]. I had a chance to pitch, and any kid in uniform would love to do that. And I got a chance to go out there in important situations.

CRAIG SWAN: As a pitcher, I had one year - especially in '78, when I led the league in earned run average - that was a funny year. It was a tough one for me, because at the All-Star break, I had a 2.50 ERA, and I pitched so many indecisions - because we couldn't score - my record was 1-5 at the All-Star break. So that was frustrating. Thankfully, I had a good second half, so I got eight more wins and finished with nine wins [and an ERA of 2.43]. Someone told me I was the second pitcher in the history of baseball who was a starter to win the earned run average and not win more than ten games. [Laughs] So I have a few of those "dubious" type records.

JOHN STEARNS: After Seaver left, Craig was our best pitcher. He was our #1 starter. And he had two or three really good years. A young guy, but he established himself as a good pitcher in the league. And he did a great job. He went out there, I think he got hurt a little bit around '79/'80 - I'm not sure what happened exactly, I can't remember - but I thought for a couple of years there, he was one of the better pitchers in the league. He had a 90+ fastball, and a hard, sweeping slider. He was a power type of guy, that would go after you in and out with the fastball and a power slider. Basically, kind of a "two pitch guy." He did have a changeup, but it was his third best pitch. He did a great job for a few years - I thought he was a legitimate #2 or #3 starter on a big league club.

PAT ZACHRY: He was just throwing hard as could be. He had real good stuff, worked hard, was getting the attention that he needed to in the training room and things were working well for him, and he was having a really good year.

CRAIG SWAN: Everything kind of came together for me [in 1978]. I had a few years under my belt. Learning the hitters took me two to three years, and then I went crazy during the winter and got myself in shape like I never have. That was because I broke my elbow in '74, and then the winter of '74/'75, I started this weight-lifting program with a guy out in Arizona, who was involved with Arizona State - that's where I went when I was in college. I started working out to the point where my age was just right - I got stronger than I've ever been. Not bulky. That's what I think is happening to some of the players today - they're getting a little too much musculature put on their bodies, and that's why they get hurt more than we used to. I think they're *too* strong.

      But I just really got myself in shape, everything was coming together, I was launching the ball well. I was hitting spots. I was always a pretty good control pitcher - I didn't walk many hitters. That season, it just all came together, and I only had one bad start that whole year. It was a fun contest, because there was a guy named Steve Rogers, who was pitching for the Expos - he and I were going into the last two weeks as the top National League earned run guys. In fact, I talked to him a few years ago about it, and I didn't see him pitch those last two weeks of that season. So I kind of had to figure out my numbers - "OK, he's got this, I'm going into the last start, if I give up less than two runs in seven innings, then I've got the earned run average thing." And I just remember going out there and was able to do that. And when I walked off the field, I knew I won that. That's a memory I'll keep.

JOHN STEARNS: Well, the big thing about Parker [a game at Three Rivers Stadium on June 30th, which saw a violent home plate collision between the Pirates' Dave Parker and Stearns] was this - there was one out in the bottom of the ninth, and we had a one-run lead. Parker was on third. There was a medium/short fly ball to right. It wasn't too short. Youngblood was out there, and he had a really good arm. So they hit the ball, and I knew they were going to send Parker to score, even though Youngblood had a good arm, it was an opportunity - they were going to make Youngblood throw him out. Parker had already knocked a couple of catchers out - put them on the DL. Steve Yeager he put on the DL [on August 24, 1977] and somebody else.

So here comes Parker. Youngblood caught the ball. It was Astroturf, so you get a good hop off the turf. Here comes the ball, and it was just up the first base line. I had to move over about four feet from home plate to catch the ball on one hop. So I caught the ball, and I immediately dove to my left, I dove on top of the plate. I've got two knees straddling the plate and the ball in my glove - reaching out to make the tag. I didn't know where Parker was, because I had to watch in right field the throw coming in. But I knew the game was on the line, so I dove on top of the plate like that, and when I looked up, Parker was maybe four feet from me, running full speed, and he wasn't sliding - he was going to try to *cremate* me.

So I had the ball in time, and I got down low, I stuck the ball up with two hands to tag him, I kind of turned my head the other way - because I didn't have a mask on, I threw that away. And he hit his cheek right on the back of my...you know the top part of your skull right up here where if you bang on it, it's really hard back there? At least mine is! He put his cheek right there. He hit me right in the head with his cheek. I went flying about 20 feet. I ended up on my back, behind home plate, after he hit me - I had the ball and I showed the umpire I had the ball. It was a double play - Youngblood made the catch and threw Parker out, and we won the game by one run [a final score of 6-5]. I got up and slammed the ball down, because Parker tried to hurt me. And I saw him lying there, moaning, holding his cheek, and then we walked off the field.

Our bench came out and got ready to fight, because I didn't see the play, but they were upset about what Parker tried to do. It must have looked like he was trying to kill me or something. But I got right up, slammed the ball down, and started walking right off to the dugout, and all my guys were coming out there, like they were going to fight somebody. As soon as I did that, everybody just relaxed, and we walked the other way. And that was it. I was lucky - the thing about that play was I had the ball in time and I was able to protect myself. Had I not had the ball, had I been trying to catch the ball when he hit me, he would have killed me.

PAT ZACHRY: I had a decent start to the season in '78, and then kicked a helmet, missed it, and broke my foot [on July 24th, after giving up a hit to Pete Rose, which tied the NL record of a 37 consecutive game hitting streak].

BOBBY VALENTINE: We were watching history. We were participating in games with the all-time hit leader, who was thinking about going after Joe DiMaggio, and if anybody was going to get a hit a game for 56, most people in that era thought that Pete was as good a bet as anyone.

PAT ZACHRY: The tough part was giving up the hit when I wanted to be the one to stop his hitting streak. He was my friend - he took good care of me, and his family did, my rookie year. I had an old dog, and Pete had two kids and no animals at home, he said, "Just bring him on over," and his wife, Karolyn, was just as good as gold, and said, "Bring the dog over here."

   We'd look up when we pulled up to the jet run when we'd come home from road trips, and Karolyn had had the old dog hanging out the window of Pete's Rolls Royce, getting dog hair all over everything! He used to tease me about how the dog had taken a shit in the back of his Rolls Royce...well, I mean, the dog didn't do *that*, but he did shit all over the place.

   He was good, Karolyn was good to me - they took good care of me and did a lot of things. Saved me a lot of money, whenever we'd go on the road. I always looked up to Pete in that regard. That's why it made it a whole lot worse to see him have problems, but it is what it is. [After breaking his toe, Zachry would not pitch again during the 1978 season - which was shaping up to be his breakout year as a Met, as he was voted to the All-Star Game that year]

CRAIG SWAN: It was me [who gave up Rose's NL record-setting hit in his 38th consecutive game, the following night]. Pete hit me like...he loved hard-throwing right-handers. He'd spray that ball to left center as good as anybody off a hard pitch. The only thing that I really remember, there was such a ceremony because we had Tommy Holmes working for us in the front office, and he had held the record for consecutive hits in the National

League [set in 1945, when Holmes played for the Boston Braves].

So Tommy was there working for the Mets, and he came on the field and they had this big presentation in the middle of the inning, right after he got the hit. I was standing out there for about five minutes, and I said, "Gee...*I'm starting to get a little cold,*" and it went on. So I left the mound, went into the dugout, got dried off in a new shirt, and had to wait for the ceremony to get over, before I took the mound again. I didn't mind giving up the hit to Pete! [Rose's record would stretch to 44 consecutive games, before ending on August 1st, with the Atlanta Braves' Gene Garber pitching]

DAN NORMAN: I know a few of the guys came over from other teams. Willie Montañez, Dock Ellis...so there was a lot of changeover at that time.

JERRY KOOSMAN: Two bad years in a row and our ballclub certainly wasn't showing any signs of getting better quickly. They had to go through a long rebuilding process. And gosh, at that stage, I was thirty-something years old. I didn't want to go through that many years with a losing record constantly. So I figured if was playing for a bad ballclub, I might as well come home and play for the Twins - in my home area. And so eventually, I was traded to the Twins [on December 12, 1978, for Greg Field and a player to be named later, which turned out to be Jesse Orosco]. The next year, '79, I won 20 with the Twins [20-13]. And I was still throwing the same way I was throwing in '77 and '78, but I had some good run support in '79.

BOBBY VALENTINE: Dr. James Parkes, who was the [Mets'] surgeon, thought he could surgically repair my messed up ankle. So I went through an operation [circa '77/'78], trying to regain some flexibility.

PAT ZACHRY: I remember people like Dr. Parkes [the Mets' team physician from 1974-1991], who unfortunately is no longer with us. That really tore my wife and I up - he was one of the nicest people I think I ever met, related to the game. To learn of his passing years ago [in 1999], was really a disappointment. Just a super nice man - I wish guys like him and Tom McKenna [the Mets' head trainer from 1970-1980] were still alive. I haven't seen or heard from [trainer] Larry Mayol - he's another fantastic person that was with us.

BOBBY VALENTINE: I got released in spring training of the '79 season [on March 26th]. I was fooling myself at the time, and I was a little disappointed, only because I had a lot of good friends on the team. Joe and Eddie Kranepool were about the same age, and I was younger, but not as young as some of the young guys. So I thought I was going to be able to hang on another year.

PAT ZACHRY: Just a tough year [1979], trying to come back the next season, and it was horrible. Nothing went right that year.

STEVE HENDERSON: I tore my ankle up. I don't know what year [1979] - I hyper-extended my ankle. It was rough.

PETE FALCONE [Mets pitcher from 1979-1982]: The bright spot back in '79 when I came to spring training, we had Lee Mazzilli. Lee and I were friends, and we played against each other in high school. We played together on sandlot teams, and Lee was a "first round/bright spot pick." He was the bright spot of our team. And rightly so, because at the time, the Mets needed somebody - a hometown boy - to come out and do what he did. And he had a good year that year.

GARY "BABA BOOEY" DELL'ABATE: Lee Mazzilli...the team sucked, and we got to send one guy, and that he sort of shined on the national stage was a big deal [at the 1979 All-Star Game on July 17th, Mazzilli hit a game-tying home run in the eighth inning, and drew a bases-loaded walk that resulted in the go-ahead/eventual winning run in the ninth...yet Dave Parker was awarded MVP]. If I'm correct in my memory, they had to let you send at least *one* player - each team had to be represented by one player. I would love to see from like, 1975 to 1982...I would bet the farm that the Mets never sent more than two players once!

DAN NORMAN: I remember they traded José Cardenal from the Phillies to the Mets [on August 2nd] during a game. One minute, he's over in the Phillies' dugout. And then the second game of the double header, he's in our dugout! [Laughs]

JEFF REARDON [Mets pitcher from 1979-1981]:   I was very nervous [coming up to the Mets and pitching]. They had some pretty big veterans - Craig Swan the year before was the ERA champ, John Stearns, Kranepool was there. So I was a little starstruck. And even though they were a last place team, they had some good players that turned out to have pretty good careers.

PETE FALCONE: I don't remember what the attitude was. I don't know the mindset of the organization. I was new to the organization, so to me, it was like, "OK, new team, let's go out there and try to do my best." I don't remember what the "talk of the town" was at the time. All the good pitchers were gone, like Tom Seaver and Jerry Koosman and Nolan Ryan. Those days were gone now. We had a lot of young guys on the team at the time. We had some good veterans - I remember Willie Montañez was on the team. But if you look at the division back then - the

National League East - it was a pretty powerful division. I mean, you had Pittsburgh, St. Louis, Philadelphia, and Montreal. It's hard to beat those teams, day in and day out. I think if I remember correctly, that was the toughest division in baseball at the time.

I know the American League East was tough, with the Yankees, the Orioles, and the Red Sox - that was always a tough division. But the National League East back then, it was like, *"Oh man."* It was a tough division, and I thought the Expos were the best team in the division! I'm not putting down Pittsburgh, Philadelphia, St. Louis, or even Chicago, but we did not have a team to overcome any of those teams, day in and day out. We did beat them - I think I beat every team in the division that year - but they're going to beat us three out of four or two out of three, *every time.* We didn't have the depth or the talent to compete with that thing. The line-ups those teams had were sometimes pretty tough to pitch to, or unbearable. And I think at the time, if I remember, the Mets were in a transition time with selling the team. It was tough.

And I'm telling you, there were some games at home we played, there was *nobody* in the stands. Oh my goodness gracious. I remember a game one time - and I know I'm not exaggerating - I went out to pitch a first game of a twilight double header, it was in 1979, probably in late September. Usually in the end of the season, that's when you could make up all of your rainout games. At the time, that's the way it was. When I went out there, against the Chicago Cubs, I think I got knocked out in the second inning, there was absolutely nobody at the stadium watching the game - but maybe ten people, and the ushers waiting for people to come in, so they could pass out peanuts and popcorn. And believe me when I tell you this - I don't even think I'm exaggerating. I remember going out there and taking the mound, and looking in the stands, and I'm going, "This is not even like spring training here. This is New York City - Shea Stadium. *What is going on here?"* I think by the time that first game ended, there was maybe a few hundred people in the stands.

JEFF REARDON: In the minor leagues, you're not going to have crowds anywhere. Not that the Mets had a lot, but it was "Game of the Week" [on August 25th] - back then, they had one game a week, and we were on against the Big Red Machine, the Reds. And they call me in I think the seventh inning - they were probably saving Neil Allen for the last. I got the first two guys out - I was pretty pumped up. And then Johnny Bench came up, and he flared one to right field for a double, and then George Foster came up. I think that was one of his big years - 40/50 home runs [Foster hit 30 homers in '79, after coming off hitting 52 homers in '77 and 40 homers in '78].

I blew two by him, and then I wind up trying to blow another one by him, and he fouled it off, and the bat broke and stuck in the umpire's throat! Ed Montague was the umpire. After that situation is where they came out with the thing that hangs down there [from the umpire's mask]. So I'm standing on the mound - I'm just a rookie, I'm nervous as hell. When I say "big crowd," there may have been 20,000, but that was a lot in those years at Shea Stadium. And I'm standing out there - the catcher ain't coming out to me, and we had to wait until they got a new umpire. *No one's talking to me, and we're facing the Big Red Machine.* So, I just wait there, and when the umpire's ready, I come back and try to blow another one by him, and he hit it over the goddamned scoreboard. [Laughs] So that put them up, I got the last out, and we wound up losing [by a score of 8-4].

PETE FALCONE: Craig Swan hurt his arm one year. And I remember this like yesterday - it was the last game of the season in 1979 [actually, the second-to-last game of the season, on September 29th]. I was supposed to pitch in St. Louis, and we had lost 99 games, and Joe Torre didn't have the confidence in me to win. He thought, "We've got one game left. I've got my best pitcher here who can pitch on three days rest." So he stuck Swanie out there instead of me. And that's the day that Craig Swan hurt his arm. And Craig Swan was never the same after that.

SKIP LOCKWOOD: I really wanted to stay [Lockwood was granted free agency on November 1st, and eventually signed with the Boston Red Sox]. Tom Seaver had convinced me to buy a home in Greenwich, and we wanted to stay. It was all my intention to stay in New York and be part of the Mets ongoing. I never got to talk to anybody, nor was there anybody to negotiate with. The ownership was changing. I notified them that I was going to seek free agency - nobody even called me back. So it was kind of a strange turn of events in '79 to '80 in New York for me. It would have been my great desire to stay in the area. We loved New York and we loved Greenwich, Connecticut.

PETE FALCONE: It was a bad time. You know what? *We sucked.* As a team, we were terrible. And it wasn't only the team - it was the whole organization. From the top down. Everybody wants to bash the team, but you know what? The front office stunk, too. Those were losers too - just like we were. And I'm not ashamed to say that. But we had some good players, and all those bad years for the Mets turned out to be good, because they got some good draft picks after that.

CHAPTER 5:
NEW OWNERSHIP &
1980

CRAIG SWAN: That was exciting [when Nelson Doubleday Jr. and Fred Wilpon became co-owners of the Mets, on January 22, 1980]. I had been with the team since '73, and saw the direction that the old ownership was going, and when they sold to Doubleday and Wilpon, that was an exciting time. I knew the team was going to change. I didn't know how long it was going to take, but I knew they were going to put some time and effort and money into it.

JOHN STEARNS: I think that the Wilpons were good, and you got M. Donald Grant out of there, and the Paysons were out. You had a younger type of owner, that I think was more in tune with what was going on at the time.

STEVE JACOBSON: The landmark exchange to me was when Frank Cashen came from Baltimore [Cashen served as the Mets' General Manager from 1980-1991]. He had an eye for people who were judges. He's the guy that traded Milt Pappas for Frank Robinson, who was then in Cincinnati, called "an old 30." And Cashen saw much more in there and made that deal, and actually created - to me - the best team that I had seen in 50 years.

CRAIG SWAN: Frank Cashen had been around longer - he had more experience than Joe McDonald did. And I think Joe Mac was under the gun of M. Donald Grant, so he didn't get to do "GM type stuff," because Grant was so involved with everything, he was kind of more like a puppet. So Grant kind of ran everything, and Joe was under that regime, so he just had to do what he could to keep his job. But again, if we weren't going to go for free agents - like they did with Cashen - Joe Mac didn't have a chance. And he couldn't produce anything unless they were willing to spend some money, so they weren't.

PETE FALCONE: I remember we were in spring training, and it was kind of bizarre [that there was a possibility of a strike - which resulted in the final eight games of the 1980 spring exhibition schedule being cancelled]. We had gone through almost the whole spring training, and I'm sitting there going, "Wow, what are we going to do here?" It was almost time to break camp and go home. And I think we were like a week a way. As a matter of fact, Neil Allen and I drove back to New York together, and we got back to New York, and we got ready for the season, and we didn't know what to do. There was no communication with nobody. [A strike in 1980 would ultimately be avoided when an agreement was met between players and owners on May 23rd - on everything except free agency, which would ultimately result in a lengthy strike in 1981]

JEFF REARDON: I remember I pitched a lot of games that year and had a great ERA, and I was really getting to feel like a sort of, so-called "veteran," and I really wanted to stay there. I was from Massachusetts - which isn't too far away. My family got to come down a lot. I was looking forward to having a long career with the Mets. I remember in 1980, guys like Mark Bomback...kind of a marginal pitcher, but still won some games. We looked like we were going to be a lot better team.

PAT ZACHRY: Hit him in the rear end [is what Zachry recalls about what sparked a fight with the Dodgers' Ron Cey during a game on June 10th]. He had hit a home run I think, was trying to come inside, and he didn't move, and the ball moved about two or three feet and ran in on him, and hit him right in the butt. So he was yelling at me, "Don't hit me anymore," and I'm yelling at him, "Hey, if you're going to stand up there, you've got to give a little room." He didn't like it and came running out there, and the next thing you know, we've got both benches going. And if I remember correctly, we came back and won the game [by a score of 5-4]. In fact, we played pretty well from that point on with them.

PETE FALCONE: I remember that [on August 13th, the Mets were only a game below .500 and 7.5 games behind the first place Phillies, until the Phillies came to Shea and swept five games from the Mets from August 14th-17th]. I remember for some reason, we put something together. It was almost like a Cinderella time. I'm not sure how long it lasted - we just got hot. But that five game series, I was banished to the bullpen. I don't think I got in any one of those five games, if I remember correctly. Maybe I came in mopping up one game, I don't know. But they just came to town and took us down. That was the year they won the World Series. [The Mets never recovered from the Phillies series, eventually resulting in a twelve game losing streak from August 31st-September 12th]

STEVE HENDERSON: We were playing pretty good in the division, and all of a sudden, stuff just happened. Stearns wound up breaking his finger, and it hurt us pretty bad.

JOHN STEARNS: Did I have an injury in 1980? I believe I had an injury. I had a broken finger - I got a foul tip, and was out the last two months. I had a good season going that year, and I had a foul tip break my finger on July 26th, and I missed the last two months. We made a run at it, we were pretty close - I remember we were in the pennant [race]. And I was kind of out of there for August and September, and we ended up falling back. I was out for the year, had surgery, and even came back the next spring training and my finger was still bothering me. I have a really ugly looking finger on my hand - to this day.

CRAIG SWAN: I do not [have a memory of the season-changing Phillies series], and you know why? Because I tore my rotator cuff that year mid-season. And Dr. Parkes didn't want me to work out, so I was kind of devastated after I tore it. So I don't think I went to any games, because I was useless - I think I was still on the roster, but I couldn't even practice. When I tore the rotator cuff he basically says, "Don't use your arm," and he was going to put me in a sling for nine months. So I kind of rested at home and I watched it on TV. But I don't have any memory of the Phillie thing.

PAT ZACHRY: We fell flat on our faces [against the Phillies]. I just remember they beat us and we were all standing around looking at each other like, *"What in the hell did we just do?"* I mean, it was really crazy. We were very excited about getting a chance to play them, and then we fell just completely flat on our faces. We couldn't do anything right in that series. When it was finished, we were all kind of pointing fingers at ourselves - and there were a couple of big mouths in the clubhouse who were doing most of that, without going into names. For me, it was time. I knew it right then and there - *that's it.* It just got to where everything had worn out its welcome.

CRAIG SWAN: Great fielder [is how Swan describes Doug Flynn, who won the Gold Glove Award for NL second baseman in 1980 - one of the few positive accomplishments for the Mets that season]. As good as any fielder. Just a light hitter. I always asked Torre if I could hit in front of Doug, because I thought I was a better hitter. [Laughs] He wouldn't do it, though.

GARY "BABA BOOEY" DELL'ABATE: Yeah, a Gold Glove at second base is going to get you to a World Series! That's like saying, *"And the other guy had a perfect attendance record that year."*

CHAPTER 6:
1981

RANDY JONES: My first thought was it was a great blend of veteran guys [Jones was traded to the Mets from the Padres on December 15, 1980, for Jose Moreno and John Pacella]. And they had pretty much the nucleus - we had John Stearns behind the plate, we had Mazzilli, Mookie Wilson got a little bit of playing time, Rusty Staub, Joel Youngblood. A lot of pieces were there, but I was a little bit worried - I thought our pitching staff was not as good as it should have been, probably. You had Pat Zachry, Craig Swan, myself, Pete Falcone, but it was just a crazy year anyway, with the strike and everything else in the middle of the season.

STEVE HENDERSON: They made a trade [to the Chicago Cubs, on February 28, 1981] for a fellow by the name of Dave Kingman! I wasn't so much disappointed, I was just sad to leave them guys there, because it was my first Major League team - with the Mets. It kind of hurt me a little bit, because I wanted to stay there, to see if we could make something really happen around there. But I understand the business of the game.

JOHN STEARNS: We had Dave Kingman and Rusty Staub [the latter re-signed with the Mets as a free agent on December 16, 1980] - we had some veteran players back in there. They started getting rid of some guys - Henderson was gone by then, and Flynn may have been traded shortly after that [after the '81 season]. In '80, '81, and '82, it seemed like we started to compete a little better - even though the record may not show that. I thought we started to get better.

PETE FALCONE: Rusty became like the "player rep/captain." Rusty was a great hitter - people don't realize what a good hitter he was. He was a pinch-hitter and he played some first base. Rusty and I used to go jogging together. I always liked Rusty.

RANDY JONES: Dave Kingman was always a home run threat, and a positive guy around the clubhouse and around the field, in my opinion. He could get a little moody here and there, but y'know, *welcome to baseball.* I thought overall, he was a pretty good veteran guy to have around there. And Rusty Staub, I think if you look up "gamer," you'll probably see Rusty's name there. He came to play every day that he was in the line-up, and a real good clubhouse guy - as far as the young kids and stuff. He was having problems with shin splints and everything else that year - really struggling. But he still went out there and gave you everything he had. He hit over .300 that year [Rusty hit .317 in 1981]. It was something else to see the veteran guys around.

PETE FALCONE: Randy Jones was a great pitcher with the Padres. He was dynamic. I think in '75 and '76 - he was as good as there was in the league. When he came to New York, he wasn't the same. He didn't have that biting sinker and that sharp slider. He was kind of on his way out, if I remember correctly. I don't even think he pitched that much that year.

RANDY JONES: My two years [with the Mets], the frustrating part is that I couldn't stay healthy.

CRAIG SWAN: I was still rehabbing. I was in that nine-month wait, so I don't even think I went down to spring training that year. I couldn't do anything - he didn't even want me to run. [Laughs] So I don't have much memory of that, either. It's a funny story - I was down in that nine-month wait, and I was about seven months into it, and I was going crazy up in Connecticut. I had a friend down here in Florida - a sailing friend, actually. We both had small catamarans on the beach on Treasure Island, and he owned the home, so he let me park my little catamaran.

I came down from Connecticut, and I said, "I'm just going to go sailing," and he saw me pulling my sail up with my left arm. He said, "Craig, what's wrong?" And I said, "Well Paul, I've got a torn rotator cuff." And he said, "Have you ever tried rolfing?" I said, "What did you say?" And he said, *"Rolfing."* I said, "Well, what's rolfing, Paul?" And he made a motion with his hands, like he was kneading dough, and he said, "Well, they kind of do this to you, and they teach you things." And I looked at him, and I said, "Well, what do they teach you, and what the heck was that you were doing with your hands?"

So the very next day, he took me to his rolfer in Tampa, Florida, and I think with the rolfing that I got over the next year and the efforts that I made with Larry Mayol, our trainer at Shea Stadium, because Larry and I would meet every morning throughout the off-season - every morning we could - and he would take me through strengthening exercises that we were inventing for the rotator cuff. Many are still used today, but Larry invented them - especially with the use of the...I don't even know if this machine is around anymore, the Cybex Machine. The combination of Larry Mayol and the rolfing I think let me be the first pitcher to come back from that injury.

And of course, at the end of my career, in '85, when the Angels let me go the last day of spring training, when I was coming home to New York from LA, I was at LAX, and I picked up the phone and called the Rolf Institute. I was very interested in learning this technique, and for the next couple of years, I spent in Boulder, and I did this technique for people in Connecticut for 28 years, before I came to Florida last year [2014]. I was a certified rolfer.

JEFF REARDON: Until whenever the trading deadline was back then [Reardon and Dan Norman were traded from the Mets to the Montreal Expos, in exchange for Ellis Valentine, on May 29th]. I was traded before the strike, because my father died during the strike - I remember being home. There were rumors of me or Neil getting traded. I think they realized that we both could be closers. Of course, I wasn't getting a chance. I think I may have had six saves or a couple of saves - I don't remember. But I didn't feel that I would be traded, because my stats were much better than Neil's - not counting the saves, of course. I think I had a lifetime ERA with the Mets of 2.60 or 2.70.

I actually spent two full years there, and they don't ever ask me to come out and do anything [in the modern day] - because they don't want people to remember me, because they were foolish to trade me. I was definitely traded before the strike, because my dad died right after the strike, and then [the Expos' then-manager] Dick Williams…I had to go home twice, because he was going to die immediately, and Dick let me go home. But then years later, he ripped me in his book for going home! "Excuse me Dick, *my dad's dying here."*

I was shocked the night I got traded - I couldn't believe it. I knew Ellis Valentine was a five-tool player, but if he had done what he was capable of, I think it would have been a fair trade. But I think he came up with other problems once he got to the big city of New York.

DAN NORMAN: They had sent me back down to Triple A one-year, and what had happened was I went to winter ball and did really well in Puerto Rico. I led the league in hitting in Puerto Rico in winter ball, but they didn't give me the batting title. [Laughs] But anyway, I did real well, then they brought me back to camp, and I did real well again in spring training, and they sent me down - the last day of spring training. Later on in the season, they traded me to the Expos - Jeff Reardon and I. So I went to Triple A with the Expos at that time in Denver, and then the next year, they called me to the big leagues.

JOHN STEARNS: '81 I was still out at that beginning of the year, and I eased back in there. We had a good year. We had the strike, so I didn't play a lot of games that year. But I thought we competed pretty well.

PAT ZACHRY: The biggest part of that is that I had signed a contract - a five-year contract [on January 30th, for $2 million]. Health was not the issue, it was just trying to stay with a good team in New York. We signed the contract and moved to Connecticut. My wife was eight months pregnant.

The night that the strike was in place, I had pitched that night against Cincinnati, and I drove home, and Sharron was having her labor pains, and I started writing down the times and I believe I pitched seven or eight innings that night, and I made it until about 2:30 or 3:30 in the morning, and I had to go get my mother, who was in a trailer parked in our driveway. She came in and stayed with my wife for a while, and then finally, at 10:30, they woke me up - let me sleep that long and we drove into Manhattan and had the baby that late afternoon.

My son was born in Manhattan that first day of the strike [June 12th]. We were able to get used to him and it was just a great thing. He fit into a little papoose thing that we had, and every day we'd take a walk up into the woods. It was just an idyllic time to have your firstborn son. Your firstborn child is a son and you take him and you can go for walks in the woods every day and just relax - it was a wonderful, wonderful time.

RANDY JONES: It was just very, very frustrating. I was having some arm problems already when the strike started. I took the rest, but it just went on and on and on. I tried to stay in New York - I had my family with me. But then finally, after a couple of weeks, it felt like it was going to be a long, drawn-out affair. I had my truck with me, so I loaded my family up and took off going out west. I figured if we resolved it, that I would just catch a plane wherever we were at and come back to New York, and my wife and my girls could come on back to the west coast. And it turned out, I probably took ten or twelve days cruising around. First, I went by Milwaukee and saw Rollie Fingers and his family, got done there in three or four days, so I drove down to St. Louis and saw Gene Tenace and his family, went through Midland-Odessa and saw my grandma and grandpa.

Then I finally got home, and I think I was home ten days or two weeks before they settled it, and I flew back to New York. It was just craziness - it was right in the middle of the season, trying to play catch and stay in somewhat pretty good shape. It wasn't really that hard - I did a pretty good job of that. I just remembered we played two or three exhibition games after the strike, and we went up and played Toronto in Toronto in an exhibition game. I was going to get a couple or three innings in of work. It was raining and it was wet, and I'll be danged if a groundball came back to me, and my foot slipped and I just concaved on my ankle, and blew my ankle out - before I pitched an inning after the strike. I could not believe it. So I was laid up right from the get-go when we came back. It was just a frustrating year - it really was.

PETE FALCONE: All I remember is it was a sinking feeling in your stomach. Because at the time, I remember it had happened a few times - in 1976 there was a strike in spring training, if I remember correctly. I remember going out of spring training, and there was no baseball, and we all worked out. I was working out with guys in the American League and different teams were all on some baseball field down somewhere in Florida, and we had these workouts, like we had regular spring training workouts, and there was no accountability - it was just guys getting together like on a sandlot. We met in some stadium. I forget where it was.

And Joe Torre was there and Jerry Koosman, and we're all on different teams - I'm on the Cardinals, and there were Pirates down there, there were Phillies and Expos. And we're all just mingling around, taking batting practice. Maybe even Tom Seaver was down there, and we had these meetings in the dugout. At the time, I was too young and naïve to really know what was really going on. I just wanted to play baseball. I didn't even understand what was really happening - all bargaining agreements and all this stuff. I just wanted to play. I was 21 years old at the time, and I'm like, *"I'm just happy to be here."* [Laughs]

CHARLIE PULEO [Mets pitcher from 1981-1982]: I think our record the second half may have been over .500 or close to it [24-28]. When I joined the team in St. Louis, I pitched about ten innings I think - ten or thirteen innings at the end of the year. But I think we were eliminated during that series - I think it was with Chicago.

RANDY JONES: The second half, when we came back, everybody had a little bit better attitude - it was almost like maybe the rest was good for everybody. We came back, and everybody was a little bit healthier and everybody gelled really well. We played some good baseball after the strike, I thought.

CHARLIE PULEO: Oh yes, absolutely [in response to if the Mets were still in the pennant race when he joined the team in September]. In fact, I started a ballgame - I think it was against the Cubs at the end of the year, and went eight innings and pitched real well. Bob Gibson [the Mets then-pitching coach] - who hadn't talked to me the whole time I was there - when I walked off the field after that game, him and Joe Torre told me, "If we play in the playoffs, you're pitching the first ballgame."

PAT ZACHRY: It was a tough year again, because we got close and then we faded again. But other than my son being born, there was not really that much to remember.

CRAIG SWAN: We saw [Torre being fired on October 4th] coming. We had so many bad years there. And it was time for a change.

RANDY JONES: Joe's a good manager, but it didn't match up good with the veterans and the young guys. I didn't think it was a good fit. I love Joe to death, but I wasn't surprised they moved on and hired George Bamberger [who was named the Mets' manager on October 20th].

PETE FALCONE: That was stupid. I mean, what are you firing Joe Torre for? Joe Torre, what's he supposed to do with that team? Even when I was in Atlanta with Joe Torre, they fired Joe Torre. Why? What did he do? They won the division in '82, they should have won it in '83, and '84 we could have won the division. It was just a lot injuries and stupid trades. But when they got rid of Joe, it was like, "What? Why?" There was no problem there. And they replaced him with George Bamberger. George was an American League manager for a long time - or coach, if I remember correctly - with the Orioles. He didn't bring nothing to that team.

JOHN STEARNS: I didn't see it coming. I don't know why Joe Torre was fired. Probably because he had been there five years and we hadn't won. But it wasn't Joe's fault. I thought he did a great job that whole time.

PAT ZACHRY: It did [come as a surprise]. I didn't know George Bamberger, but at the time, it was like, "Well, if that's what they got to do, then that's what they got to do. Let's see what this other guy can bring to us."

CHAPTER 7:
1982

JOHN STEARNS: They brought George Foster in on a $10 million contract for five years, which was a huge contract at that time [Foster was traded to the Mets on February 10th, in exchange for Alex Treviño, Jim Kern, and Greg Harris].

CHARLIE PULEO: I think so [that expectations were high for the 1982 Mets]. I think with a new group of coaches, and George Bamberger was in there, and the team they put together with George Foster, I thought they really had the makings of a pretty good club. Ron Gardenhire and myself were named the "Johnny Murphy Award" for spring training - the outstanding rookie players. We both made the team that spring, and I think Gardy started out at shortstop, and I started off in the bullpen and worked my way into the rotation early in the year. We got off to a good start - we were playing really well. And then we had a few games snowed out in Philadelphia early in the year.

RANDY JONES: It was pretty exciting [being the Mets' opening day pitcher in 1982]. That year, I think we were supposed to open up at home, and we got snowed out like, three days. And I was the #4 starter at that point in time, so my day fell on that, and George said, "You're going to open up in Philadelphia," so I said, "OK." That's how I ended up being the opening day pitcher, if I remember right. And it was pretty good. I didn't get a decision, it was cold and snowy on that opening day, but I went six innings and didn't give up any runs, and got out of a bases loaded jam with nobody out to end the fifth inning. I was excited about it. I'd done that about four or five times for the Padres on opening day, but to be able to do that again and keep us in the ballgame, I was very pleased.

I got off to a pretty good start in the first few months. Boy, I felt great. In fact, I won a couple of games on the road - I shut out Houston there [2-0, on May 23rd], and the start before I think I beat San Francisco [it was actually Cincinnati, when the Mets beat the Reds 7-4 on May 18th]. Actually, when I shut out the Astros and went nine innings, I was "National League Player of the Week," that week, and really feeling good about myself. Of course, the very next start, in the fourth inning, I snapped that nerve again. And that was the one that "broke my back." That just crushed me, that really did. It just seemed like after that, I rehabbed and tried to come back, but I was pretty much "a fan" the rest of the season. I came to the realization, "Randy, you're just out of bullets." The mind wanted to do it and the legs wanted to do it, but the arm said "No."

It was actually the last start of '76 [that Jones began having arm trouble] - my 317th or 318th inning for the season. My arm was a little bit tired, but I still had good stuff. I was pitching against the Reds, and threw a slider in about the fourth inning, and something just didn't feel right. So I called John McNamara, the manager, out and said, "I'm done. I don't think I can pitch anymore." And it wasn't until five days later that I had my arm checked by the doctors, and all of a sudden I realized that I couldn't make a muscle - my bicep had disappeared! I knew there was something wrong with my elbow. I snapped a nerve in my arm and my elbow, and they couldn't fix it - it just had to regenerate. And they said, "If it regenerates you can pitch again. If it doesn't, you're done." But I was fortunate to get the years after that, that I pitched. I had some pretty productive years - nothing compared to the Cy Young year. And finally after snapping it in '81 and snapping it again in '82, the writing was pretty much on the wall.

JOHN STEARNS: I was playing third base one night, because I played some other positions. I made a throw, and I felt a twinge in my elbow. I had some pain, and it just never went away. What happened was that I didn't snap the medial collateral ligament, but I frayed it - kind of half tore it. Because it wasn't torn, the doctors didn't think I needed the ligament transplant surgery - which was Tommy John Surgery. They thought I could come back from that.

So I rehabbed that thing for two or three years, and I could never throw again without pain. Now I can throw OK - I can throw the ball. But when I would snap that ball to second base, it just hurt like hell. Later, I became a big league and minor league coach, I could throw batting practice all day long. But when I have to snap a ball hard, it just really hurts my elbow, and that's what happened. I never got a chance to play again, after that elbow injury in '82. It just all happened on one day - I made a throw, boom, I felt a twinge in my elbow, like something was unraveling in there. And then I went in, I got ice on it - I actually played with it for a month without telling anybody.

CHARLIE PULEO: We went into Philadelphia to play five games [from June 25th-June 27th, at which point the Mets were only 4.5 games out of first place] - a double header Friday, a double header Saturday, and one Sunday. We lost all five games, and that was our downfall. And once that started, we never really recovered.

PETE FALCONE: They really had our number, didn't they? *Man.*

STEVE JACOBSON: One of Bamberger's coaches was Jim Frey [who was with the Mets from 1982-1983]. And the Mets had a pitcher named Pete Falcone, and Frey once went to the mound to talk to Falcone, who was often to the point of saying, "It was God's will," when something went wrong.

And Frey went to the mound and said, *"Do you think the good Lord would mind if you threw a strike?"*

CHARLIE PULEO: We were "there" for about two months. And then, things just started to unravel.

BRENT GAFF [Mets pitcher from 1982-1984]: My debut was pretty good [on July 7th, against the San Francisco Giants at Shea]. I had a shutout going for eight innings, and then Reggie Smith hit a three-run dong on me - after Gardenhire booted a routine double-play ball to get me out of the inning [the Mets lost the game, 3-2]. That was amazing [when the Mets fans gave Gaff a standing ovation when he left the mount]. That's my highlight of the whole big league experience.

One thing that always got me, I never ran before I started. And Monbo [Bill Monbouquette, the Mets' pitching coach from 1982-1983] has got everybody running, and I'm pitching, and Monbo's saying, "No, you've got to do your 20 line-to-lines. And I said, "Monbo, I don't run the day before I pitch." And he said, *"You do here."* I remember my back hurting the whole time I was on the mound, my major league debut. I ran out of gas, and I never run out of gas - I always was pretty strong, threw nine if I could. It just messed with my mojo a little bit.

JOHN STEARNS: I was in the All-Star Game in Montreal [on July 13th]. I went and took my infield, I made several throws down to second, and it was killing me. And I never recovered from it, and my career was over two years later. It was really a tough thing for me. And before I knew it, the career was over. It was a surprise for me, because I was only 30 years old when I made this throw and my arm started hurting, and I was never really able to play again. Because I thought I had another ten years left. Without an injury, I'm sure I would have played until when I was 40 or so. All of a sudden, I was out. It was tough to take.

RANDY JONES: It was definitely one of those memories where we were all just amazed [when Joel Youngblood became the first player in MLB history to get hits for two different teams on the same day, when he was traded from the Mets to the Expos on August 4th]. One second he's with us, and all of a sudden, the next second, he's not. It was crazy! Absolute craziness. But once again, Joel, even after his playing career and coaching, he had a real knack for the game. One of the most solid guys you could build around, but I know the Mets were trying to make some moves and continue to build.

PAT ZACHRY: He still holds the record? I'll be darned! You don't see many guys get into that trade situation like that. That was a weird one.

JOHN STEARNS: What I remember is we were in Chicago, playing the Cubs in a day game, he started the game for us, and before I knew it, we whipped him out of the game. And then all of a sudden, he was gone, and we were all going, "What happened here?" And then he was traded. The next thing I knew, we were reading about him - he got on a flight [to Philadelphia], and played for the Expos. It was strange - it wasn't like he was upset, either. I think I was there on the bench, the game was going on, and all of a sudden, he said, "Goodbye," and he was out of there, and we were told he got traded. It's one of those things that happens in Major League Baseball, I guess. Something that you have to accept as a ballplayer - *anything can happen.* That certainly was a surprise, that day.

CRAIG SWAN: That'll do it! [In response to being told the Mets endured a 15-game losing streak in 1982, from August 15th-31st, which effectively killed their once promising season] I don't remember it. All the bad stuff, I try to forget.

PETE FALCONE: There was a 15-game losing streak that year, and I pitched the game that broke it. It was against the Houston Astros [on September 1st, by a score of 5-1]. That I remember pretty clearly.

CHARLIE PULEO: Late in the year, I was on the disabled list for a while. I had a little tendonitis in my shoulder and missed a little time. That might have been during that streak. But it's like any losing streak - *nothing is working.* You're not pitching well, or then you hit but you're not pitching. Defensively, I thought we were a pretty solid team year round. It got to a point where we didn't really hit the ball that well, and we didn't really pitch very well. That's no secret when you're in a streak like that. It was hard to come out of that.

RANDY JONES: It was the injuries - the middle of the line-up was dilapidated. And what I remember too, our defense was a little bit shaky at that point in time. We were giving the other team too many outs. And it wasn't like we were getting blown out every single night - we might be in a lot of ballgames. But we just couldn't get it done. We'd make an error or boot a ground ball that ended up costing us a run. It was very, very frustrating. And even that year, in the first part when we were playing so well, we had a lot of comeback wins, where we'd win games late in the game. And that kind of disappeared in that final third of the season. We lost that momentum. And a couple of injuries. And when a starting pitcher is not slamming the door like they were capable of doing…they weren't doing a good job the last half.

CHARLIE PULEO: John Stearns went down with an injury. That hurt us, because he was having a pretty good year. George Foster didn't have the kind of year they were hoping he would have [Foster finished '82 with only 13 homers and a .247 batting average, compared to his 22 homers and .295 batting average - and coming in 3rd in the NL MVP voting - in the strike-shortened previous season], and the veteran pitchers. It's hard to describe. Like they say, the cream rises to the top, and we weren't as good as we thought we were, coming out of spring training, and we finished where we probably should have.

CRAIG SWAN: We must have faded fast then! [After being told the Mets' '82 record was 65-97] If we were close at the All-Star break and still lost 97, *yow!* Oh boy.

BRENT GAFF: They took me down and decided, "You know what? You're not a starter. We're throwing you in the bullpen." So I came down and pitched good out of the pen for a little bit, and thought maybe I would get called back up in September, and I didn't. I think I pitched good for a little bit, until I figured out, "You're not going to get another shot this year," so I ended up throwing pretty bad there for a while. My heart wasn't in it - I let that get the best of me, which you shouldn't do. It's hard not to, if you get sent down.

WALT TERRELL [Mets pitcher from 1982-1984]:   In September [was when Terrell made his Mets debut, on September 18th - a game the Mets lost, 6-2, against the Cardinals]. Typical September call-up is what you could say. I was very fortunate. Hell, I was thrilled to death, are you kidding me? I wasn't sure I was supposed to there or good enough to be there, but they called me up. Hell, I think I went 0-3. Didn't pitch too badly, but didn't win any. But was fortunate enough to play with some good people and good experiences. It really helped me. "Hey, *you can pitch up here."*

But I wasn't ready yet, there is no doubt in my mind - I got sent back to Triple A the next year, and rightfully so. '82 was a great experience and very thankful to be called up in September, but then sent back down the next year. I had no qualms about it, because I knew that's where I needed to be, because I needed to pitch, and I don't think I would have gotten the opportunity if I went straight to the big leagues in '83. Very fortunate for everything that happened that September.

TOM GORMAN [Mets pitcher from 1982-1985]: Well, we were horrible. [Laughs] I always tell everybody when I showed up, we were 35 games out of first, and that's usually not a good year. That was a pretty ragtag bunch when I first got over there. I would say maybe our ace was Craig Swan, Ed Lynch was pitching a little bit at the time, Ron Darling and I had played Triple A ball together. I roomed with Walt Terrell in Triple A and also roomed with him in the big leagues, too. But it was starting to develop - the team.

BRENT GAFF: Bill Monbouquette told me, "You think these guys are your friends? Every one of these starters is trying to get you sent back down, buddy. Don't be nice to these guys - *they're sticking a knife in your back.*" And it didn't take long - about a month I lasted. I ended up 0-3 with I don't even know what kind of ERA before I got sent down. The team was bad man. We sucked.

Pat Zachry was there and he was alright, but he was going through bad times - all the pitchers were getting their asses kicked. Even Mike Scott was getting his ass kicked, and Puleo - they were the two best starters. We didn't score no runs. Unless you throw a shutout, you're getting your ass kicked. And it puts a lot of pressure on a starting pitcher, like, "Really? You can't give me a fuckin' run?"

It was just overall, but mostly the veteran pitchers didn't want me there. "What's this punk doing here?" I didn't know how to act. Nowadays, I think they kind of give you a heads up, like, "Look kid, *here's what you do.* You don't do this, you don't do that." And I just came from a real loose atmosphere in Triple A, where we're kicking everybody's butt and having fun. I was on like, a different planet when I got there. Well, it didn't take me long to fly back down to earth, that's for sure.

TOM GORMAN: When I first broke in, Randy Jones was there. And Randy and I became really good friends in the short period of time that I did spend time with him. When he retired, I would still see him in San Diego - he owned some car washes in San Diego, so when we flew into San Diego, I would spend some time with him. Randy was the one that gave me my nickname ["Fax"], actually. So I feel obligated in that regard. And people still call me that to this day, and my friends call me that around town. I thought he was a very neat guy. And he won the Cy Young in '76, so it was neat to meet him. And then other veterans, Mike Torrez was there for a short period of time [from '83-'84]. Mike would help out the younger guys, too. Ed Lynch had been around - Ed wasn't an old veteran at the time, but Ed probably had a year and half in there at the time, Jesse Orosco had been there for a little bit. So all those guys, I came up with - along with Walt and Ron Darling and Sid Fernandez and all those guys. That was the core of the staff that eventually went on to win the World Series.

It was funny, because we were out in right field, and it was my first game, and I'm sitting out there, and here comes Randy. Randy kind of looked like Papa Smurf really, when you looked at him - he was an interesting fellow. [Laughs] He comes over, and says, "Lefty, what's your repertoire?" And I said, "Well, I've got a fastball like Goose Gossage and I've got a curveball like Sandy Koufax." He'd never seen me pitch, so he walks over to centerfield and comes back, and says, "Well lefty, do you have a nickname?" I said, "No." And he says, "Well, you do now. *Your nickname is Goose Gorfax."* Obviously, no one likes to use more than one syllables in a nickname, so it went from "Goose Gorfax" to "Gorfax" to "Fax." So, my friends around here call me "Fax." And if I called Brent up right now, and said, "Gaffer, how are you doing?" He'd say,

"Fax!" Frank Howard used to call me "The Golden Goose." I don't know why he did that...

PETE FALCONE: I know George hit behind Kingman - that was probably why [Kingman lead the NL in home runs for 1982, with 37]. Kingman was Kingman. When he was on, he was tough. I remember him hitting a few balls - I remember he hit the ball in the upper, upper deck in Philly one night. I mean, when he hit a baseball, it was like something you've never seen before. But when he went bad, he went *bad.* He would look...*oof.* But when he was on, he was tough.

CRAIG SWAN: The only thing about Kong I remember is sometimes he missed the ball by a foot or two feet it looked like, and then sometimes if he hit the ball, it went farther than anybody I ever saw hit a ball. He was a very strong man. He looked kind of thin, but he was unbelievably strong. Actually, we were wrestling in the clubhouse one day, and he got behind me and picked me up in the air, turned me upside down - in the air, without me touching the ground - and then went over and stuffed me into a big old thing of towels! And I weigh 225/230. That was a strong man. But I just remember, when he got a hold of them, we loved to see "Kong shots," we called them.

CHARLIE PULEO: Dave gave you what he was capable of. He was a real nice fella. I was always glad that he was playing first base when I was out there, because I knew if there was a fight - and with Stearns behind the plate - that I would be protected! Those two guys - one's a defensive back and one's 6'6" - I could do whatever I'd want, and I'd be OK. I was always happy those guys were there. He's a big guy and hit a lot of home runs. He was our offense - him and George. And when we did win ballgames, it was because those guys were hitting.

RANDY JONES: He was phenomenal. It's a lot more fun when he's on your team, rather than watch him hit them against you! He started swinging really well and you could just tell - he was having a lot of fun and was playing with a lot of confidence [in '82]. That was the real key. He kept us in so many ballgames with all those home runs, and he gave you almost 100 RBI's [99 RBI's]. There's no doubt about it - he was the main key in that line-up. You would think with him, and if we got George Foster going a little bit, then they'd make all the difference in the world. But George just never got on track - or we might have been a little bit different.

CRAIG SWAN: Behind Joe Morgan [Swan was the runner up to "NL Comeback Player of the Year" in 1982, with a record of 11-7 and an ERA of 3.35]. Nobody had ever come back from that rotator cuff tear. Now, they come back all the time, because they've got the arthroscopic surgery perfected. But back then, we didn't have arthroscopic surgery for that injury. If you got the big surgery - which means they tear all the muscles apart to get to the deep ones, and then sew them all back together - pitchers, they can lead fairly normal lives, and play golf and such.

But no one had ever come back and pitched after that major surgery, and that was the main reason why Dr. Parkes decided not to do that surgery on me, because nobody had come back from it. He basically said, "We're going to let Mother Nature take her course, and we're not going to do anything for that arm. The way scar tissue heals, maybe the tear will fill in with scar tissue and we can always strengthen the arm later." And that's what we did.

RANDY JONES: I saw it was inevitable [Jones was released by the Mets on November 5th]. I did go to spring training with the Pirates in '83, but to no avail. My arm told me that. I think my fifth start in spring training, I knew I was going home. I definitely knew then that my arm just couldn't handle it anymore. I'd gone home, [thinking] "It was a great career." I'm not going to cry over spilled milk - I wouldn't change a thing in my playing career. And the players today, good for them - they're making money. It's well deserved, and that's why we went on strike those years - trying to create this situation. But I don't think I'd trade my years for anything. I played against some great players, met some great players, and competed against some great players. I have no regrets whatsoever.

But it was still a great time - I remember in '82, I spent a lot of time down in the bullpen. Because I couldn't really start with my arm problems, and I accepted the fact. I'd be down there with Eddie Lynch, Jesse Orosco, and Bruce Bochy was doing all the catching at that time down in the bullpen. And we had Neil Allen. We had just a bunch of crazy guys down there. There were some pretty good memories with some of those guys. Tom Hausman was *crazy!* The old days in Shea, they had that little bench right up above the right field fence, where you could sit and watch the game. I remember in the old days they had that there, and it was pretty cool to sit up there, watch the ballgame, and yell at the right fielder. Just a good bunch of guys, that's the one thing. In baseball, you have teammates, and they're friends the rest of your life. It's great to see them.

PETE FALCONE: They really didn't want me around there. I was a free agent [Falcone was granted free agency on November 10th], and I felt like I wasn't going nowhere. They weren't offering me a contract. And I said, "Let me just see what's out there." I remember the teams I really wanted to go to, I couldn't go to. I wanted to go pitch in Houston and in LA. For some reason, I loved those places. And I think Pittsburgh, Atlanta, and Toronto were the only teams that were interested in me.

Joe Torre had been in Atlanta, and the Braves were really starting to come on [finishing 1st in the NL West for '82, before losing to the eventual world champion Cardinals in the NLCS, 3-0]. They had put together some pretty good teams. I said, "Well, that's probably the best place for me to go to." Because Pittsburgh was still a good team, but they didn't have the Stargells - they weren't the same no more, y'know? That fire was gone. And I said, "Well, I don't want to go to the American League and pitch in Toronto, because what do I know about that?" So I went to Atlanta.

CHARLIE PULEO: After that rookie year in New York, I was traded in December for Tom Seaver - myself and Lloyd McClendon were traded to Cincinnati [on December 16th, along with Jason Felice]. I never heard my name mentioned at all - it was always Ed Lynch or somebody else, until I got phone calls from Frank Cashen and George Bamberger, and then the Reds' front office. It was disappointing. I was a Mets fan - I grew up idolizing Tom Seaver and Jerry Koosman and Tommie Agee and Cleon Jones. I could name the whole '69 Mets starting line-up, probably. That was the team I looked at the whole time. It was upsetting leaving New York, because that was home. But I had a good opportunity to go to Cincinnati and pitch there. It all worked out in the end, but I was disappointed leaving New York, for sure.

PAT ZACHRY: I was traded during the winter [on December 28th, to the Los Angeles Dodgers, in exchange for Jorge Orta], and that's all I know. They had so many guys, like Mike Scott, Neil Allen, Scott Holman - a lot of really good young talent. There was just a buttload of guys that were coming up. And they were going to be paying them the minimum and they were paying us a lot of money, so get rid of us and bring in the young arms. And they did well. Hell, look what they did almost immediately. So it was a good move for them.

BOBBY VALENTINE: I was a minor league instructor in '82, and spent the year as a roving instructor, and then got the promotion as a major league coach under George Bamberger in 1983.

CHAPTER 8:
1983

MIKE TORREZ [Mets pitcher from 1983-1984]: When we were there my first spring training [Torrez was traded to the Mets from the Red Sox on January 13, 1983, for a "player to be named later," which turned out to be Mike Davis], you could see some of the kids were coming around. Neil Allen was there, Rick Ownbey - guys who looked like they were up and coming, and we had the younger kids, like Dwight Gooden, that you knew were going to be good. You had Jesse Orosco, who blossomed into a terrific reliever. We had some young arms - Walt Terrell, guys like that - that came around.

Those kids had a lot of fun, they enjoyed the game. When I was there, I always tried to tell them, "Enjoy the game. Have fun, guys - that's the main thing. When you don't have fun in the game, then that's the time when teams suffer." I'd gone with teams where they didn't have any fun, guys didn't get together and didn't communicate together, and it was a struggle all season. But when you get a team that can communicate and pull together, you're going to have a championship team.

BRENT GAFF: I remember talking to Monbo, and I said, "Monbo, am I going to make this club?" And he says, "Nope. It's a numbers game, kid." And I said, "If I don't give up a run *the whole spring training,* I won't make this club?" And he says, "No," which kind of ticked me off. So they sent me down to minor league camp, and I was supposed to report back to minor league camp, and I was so pissed that I just drove straight to Tidewater, and went to the ballpark and started working out!

Well, Clint Hurdle was there, and he was there working out, and was like, "What the hell are you doing here?" He pretty much did the same thing - he was pissed. So Davey [Johnson, the Tidewater Tides' 1983 manager] told me, "Cashen was going to fine you $5,000, but I talked him out of doing that. But because you booked and didn't go down to minor league camp, you're not starting. You were going to be my #1 starter to open the season up. You're going to the bullpen." That was my punishment, and I never really got out of the bullpen after that.

TOM GORMAN: That was the year I started in Triple A. I had a pretty good Triple A season, and then got called up the middle of the way. Davey Johnson at the time was in Triple A, so I went down, Brent went down, Walt went down, and I think Darling was down in Triple A in '83 [Darling joined the Mets late in the season]. That's how we got our relationship with Davey. And then when Davey got called up and became [the Mets'] manager in '84, he kind of brought all his "boys" with him. And that was a neat thing. But I would imagine that if you looked at my stats, I bet I didn't pitch a whole lot [in '83]. I was more of a middle relief guy. I may have got a start in '83, but I doubt it. I don't think I pitched poorly - it was kind of one of those deals where I was the last guy to go in spring training of '83, and I was kind of the last guy not to go in '83 with the club, to stick.

CRAIG SWAN: I actually hurt my arm that spring training and didn't tell anybody, and tried to pitch, and didn't do very well. I tore some myofascial tissue off my tricep, that wasn't found until the Angels picked me up [next season] and sent me to have surgery, and the surgeon found it.

TIM McCARVER: They were a bad team [when McCarver joined the Mets as a broadcaster in '83]. But I really enjoyed Ralph Kiner. And Steve Zabriskie I knew a little bit with ABC - I think he learned about the game from Ralph and me, and we took a little page of his broadcasting experience. And it gelled, it worked. It was more fun than you could imagine.

RICK OWNBEY [Mets pitcher from 1982-1983]:   The day that I'll never forget was opening day 1983, when I did make the big league club, because opening day at Shea Stadium was the Mets against the Phillies - and the match-up was Tom Seaver against Steve Carlton. I just thought, "Wow. How did I get here? *This is amazing!*" [Laughs]

BOBBY VALENTINE: I remember [Seaver] walking in from the bullpen his first time back - to a full-house standing ovation, that lasted longer than most standing ovations I have ever seen in baseball. I remember him tipping his hat as he walked in. I remember driving to the ballpark with him - he lived in Greenwich, I lived in Stamford. It was great having him back.

MIKE TORREZ: With Tom being there, it was a great feeling - to have two established starting pitchers along with the younger kids coming up.

CRAIG SWAN: It was interesting - he was back with his home team. Although during the winters, we were still seeing each other - although he was playing for another team. So, I was kind of used to seeing him. It was nice to have him back on the team. He pitched well. He never hurt himself - he never had a bad arm. He'd have small leg injuries, but his arm never got hurt. He just used his body so efficiently that he wasn't going to hurt himself.

TOM GORMAN: Tom and I had an interesting relationship - you could almost call it a "love/hate relationship." He used to call me names - which I don't really want to have on record - and then I'd say, "Y'know, I used to have a lot of respect for you until I met you!" We kidded back and forth. We played gin together in spring training. I don't think it was a killer year for Tom. [Seaver finished '83 with a 9-14 record, and a 3.55 ERA]

When I broke into the big leagues [with the Montreal Expos in 1981], it was in Cincinnati I got called up. I was late for the game, but when I got up the stairs and into the dugout, there was Tom Seaver on the mound. So I always remember that. It looked like heaven when you walked up through there - it was all lit and everything, there's Tom Seaver on the mound, and remnants of the Big Red Machine at the time. I'll never forget that visual. But Tom and I had a good relationship. For a veteran, Tom wasn't one of those guys to really put his arm around a young guy and go from there. He had been around for quite a while, and we must have all looked like a bunch of youngsters to him. A bunch of dumb rookies.

RICK OWNBEY: I think Tom tried to do everything he could to pass on to make the other pitchers/players/the organization better around him. The one thing that you kind of had to watch out for was for me, was to start trying to emulate or pitch like Tom Seaver, and that's not really what you want to do. You want to take something from everyone, but you still have to be yourself and be comfortable with what you're doing. There was probably more mental make-up, maybe pitch selection and things like that, that you did, because Tom Seaver, I don't know if he was 6'0"/6'1", I was more 6'3"/195/long arms - it's just a different style or way of pitching. But still, a tremendous ball player, a tremendous teammate, and obviously, a Hall of Famer.

GARY "BABA BOOEY" DELL'ABATE: I remember being really excited that he was coming back. Listen, I didn't expect to have the same guy back, and I thought that he was getting towards the end of his career, and it was done more to tug at people's heartstrings, but I was happy to have him back and happy to see him in a Met uniform again. I didn't know they were going to be good soon. And it was heartbreaking when they let him go again [Seaver would be claimed in a free-agent compensation draft by the Chicago White Sox on January 20, 1984].

I remember I went to "Tom Seaver Day" at Shea Stadium, there was a special day they did with him [probably the pre-game ceremony on June 24, 1988, when Seaver's #41 was retired by the Mets]. Even in my basement, one of the things I have in my man-cave is a picture of him and Piazza with their backs hugging on the mound at the last day at Shea [during a post-game ceremony on September 28, 2008]. I was at that game, too! But again, the Mets let him go to the White Sox, and then he wins his 300th game there [on August 4, 1985, against the Yankees, at Yankee Stadium]. He wasn't done yet.

STEVE JACOBSON: Seaver was very smart and knew much about pitching. I wrote a book with him about mechanics of pitching for kids [1974's 'Pitching with Tom Seaver'], and as a guy, I don't know...I don't think he was great. My wife has been introduced and introduced herself to Nancy Seaver a hundred times, and Nancy still doesn't know who she is.

TIM McCARVER: I remember him as my bridge partner. [Laughs] And nobody could beat us, either! We played on the plane a lot. But I got to know Tom very well, and as a matter of fact, I visited him a couple of times at his winery - I've got a place in Napa, and he's got a lovely home near Calistoga. We visited a couple of times up there, and I've seen him in Napa several times and we became very good friends.

And of course, I think the Mets have admitted that they made a mistake dangling Tom Seaver and leaving him available to be taken in the draft in 1984. I mean...*he's Tom*

Seaver. Tom Seaver with the Mets is like Henry Aaron with the Braves, Nolan Ryan with the Astros and Rangers, and Bob Gibson with the Cardinals. He's "Tom Seaver of the Mets." Drop and drive, 300 game winner. You're looking at a Hall of Famer at a very young age. [Seaver was 47 years old when elected to the Hall of Fame in 1992 - receiving the highest-ever percentage of votes, with 98.84%]

STEVE ZABRISKIE [Mets TV broadcaster from 1983-1989]: It was a season of transition. Because '84 was the first year they were "decent," if you want to call it that. I think one of the things that the Mets did that season that was very, very intelligent, was use that '83 season as a building year. They kind of knew that they weren't going to be a contender, and instead of trying to do things like find some veteran players to make them better, they did focus on the youth they had. Because they had a pretty good farm system. They may have - on the negative side - rushed a couple of guys, in an effort to get them up and get them experienced and get them better. But I don't think they felt like they had the luxury of time, and so it was really smart to use it as a building year.

One of the things that was interesting about that was when Tim and I came in, we had not been "Mets guys," so to speak. Timmy wasn't a Mets player, neither was I. I had come from the network, Tim had come from the Phillies. So we were not really "homers" in that sense - we were very objective in what we said on the air. The management of the Mets was fine with that. We were told to just do our jobs and "call 'em as we see 'em," as the cliché goes. So we did that. And we wouldn't have done it any other way.

And it really was a bit of a shock to some people, because I think that when we were very quick to say, "That was a bad play or a mistake," or whatever criticism might have been levied - albeit honest and real - a lot of people weren't used to that. And *Ralph* wasn't used to that! We used to get some looks from Ralph in the booth. And Murph [Bob Murphy] wasn't used to that. So it was a transitional period in many ways, because the broadcast - just like the team - was transitioning from what had come before, into something that was going to be a little new and different.

TIM McCARVER: I think the date was May 6th [that Darryl Strawberry made his debut with the Mets], wasn't it? Because I believe it was Willie Mays' birthday. [McCarver is correct with both!] And leave that to Ralph to bring that up, and he did bring that up. It was really appropriate. But I have rarely seen a young talent as powerful with his swing than Darryl Strawberry. I mean, this guy had *power*...just reeked of power. And with that bat curl and everything - what an unbelievably gifted young man.

I've even said - after watching him for two or three months, and it was an easy call - "One of these days, he's going to hit the longest ball in the history of the game." And I kept saying that, too. I thought that he would. I don't believe he did, but in a home run hitting contest before the 1986 All-Star Game in Houston, he hit the back wall with the ball, and he also hit a ball that hit the top of Olympic Stadium in I believe it was 1988. It was a prodigious clout, to say the least. Had the roof not been there, that could have been the longest ball in the history of the game. [Laughs] And I'm serious about that. But it hit the rafters, so nobody had an idea, nobody knew how to gauge the distance. But that ball right there could have been...I mean, had it been in the open air or with a little wind behind it, outside, there's no telling how far that ball would have been distanced.

BOBBY VALENTINE: In the minor leagues, I remember what a wonderful talent he was. I remember his smile, his swing, and his stride. I remember working with him on his baserunning and his bunting and his outfield play. And when he got to the major leagues, there were some people that thought he wasn't ready. I thought he was ready as soon as he got there. I remember he hit the ball off the Montreal façade up at the old Olympic Stadium in right field - the same way as Kingman hit it in left field. And I saw both of those towering drives, that seemed to be superhuman.

WALT TERRELL: What an unbelievable talent - could run, throw, hit. Hit with power, hit for average, steal, could cover in the outfield, could throw…what would be not to like? Dave Parker-ish - I'm not sure to that extent, but at the time, thought of that way. Dave Parker had a pretty damn good career, pretty good player, so I remember people talking. Other than stature - Darryl was skinnier, obviously - that's what people talked about, was talent like Dave Parker. There just aren't many of those guys around. He could hit it a mile, and then he could hit a rocket to right centerfield or left centerfield, and get a triple. A different class of athlete. For a young kid - 19/20 years old - are you kidding? *Amazing.* Absolutely an amazing talent.

CRAIG SWAN: Tall, skinny guy, that could hit the heck out the ball, run, and throw. Nice kid. Really good teammate. It was just nice to see somebody with so much talent on our side.

RICK OWNBEY: There was a time where Darryl Strawberry looked like he could possibly be one of the best players to ever play the game. His build, that swing, his power, run, throw, hit, whatever you want to call it, I think at that time, if you could build a robot and go, "Here's the finished product of what we came out with," it seemed to be Darryl. He went on, and no matter how good you are, when you're in the big leagues, people are always trying to find a little pocket or hole in your swing, or go at you, or try to get you out this way or try to get into your head - they'll walk you. There's all kinds of different ways to make yourself very frustrated. I got along with him just fine - I thought he was a great ball player and I know he had some struggles [off the field], but if I'm not wrong, he's doing a lot better, and that makes me very happy.

CRAIG SWAN: I think Bambie just got tired [Bamberger abruptly left the Mets on June 3rd, with coach Frank Howard taking his place for the remainder of the season]. He was older. The travel, the whole thing - he had been in baseball his whole life. It seemed kind of natural - just that he was tired and he wanted to cash it in. That was a tough one.

BOBBY VALENTINE: George left when we were out in California, during a road trip. They [Bamberger and Howard] were the direct opposite. Frank was the most energetic, talkative - if you will, "rah-rah" - exciting type of person that you'd ever want to be around. And George was a soft-spoken guy, who as he said the day he left, that he'd rather be fishing. He was a pitching coach turned manager.

STEVE ZABRISKIE: I think they had to do *something* [the Mets were 17-30 and in last place/9.5 games out of first at the time of Bamberger's exit]. And they had to do it more for the fans more than anybody else. I think they also had to show…what a lot of people couldn't see was, "We have a plan, we're doing something, this is coming, we're building, you don't see a lot of it because it's down in Tidewater or somewhere else. But we're doing something." And to bring Frank Howard in I think was cool, because Frank was already a part of the team, and Hondo - as we call him - is just a great guy. George was a nice guy, but George wasn't one of the guys that I would categorize as being "inspirational." Bambie was a nice man, he was a very good pitching coach. But I don't know that he was what the Mets needed at that time.

I think that the change was good, because it was another one of those little steps, like bringing up Strawberry, where people can see, "Hey, we're making an effort. We have a plan, we're doing something. We're getting there." I don't know that Hondo was the answer, either, and I don't think the Mets felt that was. But I think that it did send a message, and it did make a difference in the atmosphere and the attitude of the ballclub, which was in a positive way. Because Hondo is very upbeat. He's a big presence. A big guy! And he commands a lot of notice. But he also has a very positive impact and outlook on things, and I think that was needed, because the season wasn't going anywhere, so a little better attitude didn't hurt.

WALT TERRELL: George was good to me. The first time I ran into him in spring training, I'm from Indiana, so I've got a pair of blue jeans on and a sweatshirt, and he says, "Hey, no more dungarees." I went "Yes sir," and I walked away, sitting there thinking, *"What in the hell is a dungaree?"* - because I had no idea! So I wasn't allowed to wear blue jeans after that. But treated me very well and told me the things to work on - I was too slow to home plate was the biggest thing, and I got that. I didn't throw 95 miles an hour. "You need to get another pitch here, throw strikes, and you've got a shot" - and he let me do those things. Then when Frank came on, very personable, fun to be around. Tremendous stories and just the stuff he did that I thought with the team was really good, and I thought we were playing pretty well - honestly, I thought he had a shot too at being the [permanent] manager. It didn't happen, but great baseball guy and just fortunate to be around him.

TOM GORMAN: That was a trying time again for us. I don't have our record in front of me, but I would bet you that we finished 35 games out of first [the Mets finished 22 games out of first in 1983]. So it was a trying time for everybody. I think one of the best stories - not necessarily for Frank's end of it - but we got on a plane one time, and we were heading to LA, so it was a long flight. And we had just lost a game - it was late in the season. Frank got into the wine pretty hard, and I remember Artie coming up to us -

our traveling secretary - and we had all got off the plane and onto the bus. And he went into the bus and said, "Hey, we need some guys to help Frank off the plane." So about six of us...well, the "Scum Bunch" they used to call us, went onto the plane, and Frank was dead weight. We carried him off the plane and onto the bus.

We stayed at the same hotel there that they do all the filming of movies...I want to say it was the Biltmore or something like that. But we couldn't very well carry him through the front lobby, so we had to stay on the bus, and we went around to the back, and we carried him up a freight elevator, and put him in bed. The next morning, we're at Dodger Stadium, we come up, and the first guy we see is Frank, in his usual garb - it was a jock strap and he had these dumbbells. They were heavy, and he's pumping iron, and, "Hey fellas! *How ya doin'?"* He didn't remember anything! [Laughs] But I remember everybody had a bad back - Frank was about 6'9", 320, and we had to carry him off the plane. But that's my favorite story about Frank - I tell that story all the time. It's not a great description of Frank - that doesn't happen all the time. I think he just had enough and wanted to forget about it!

But Frank was always great to me, he really was. I remember I was pitching in Chicago one time, and Darryl had got hit early, and I don't think it was on purpose or anything. But Darryl kind of had a "red ass" that day, and he's yelling, "You pitchers have to protect us hitters!" And it was that the ball got away from somebody, maybe - Sutcliffe or whoever. He was bitching about it, and Frank came out and I always felt like he was on my side. I considered Frank a good friend. He just said, "Hey, don't worry about what he says. You just pitch your game and don't worry about it." He was kind of one of those guys. He'd invite us out to the mansion where all the coaches would stay, and we'd go swimming. Frank was a good dude, he really was.

WALT TERRELL: Fortunate enough to get called up…I don't know if it was June or July [of '83], and struggled a little bit. Did well early, then struggled, and finished up 8-8, and wasn't really sure what was going to happen. I know at one time, we were in Houston, facing Nolan Ryan, and if I didn't win the game, I was going back to Triple A. And I thought, "Oh, that's great - the Mets have *never* beaten Nolan Ryan!" So that made me feel really, really good. But we played well and we won the game [on July 17th, the Mets beat the Astros 3-1]. Frank Howard was the manager at that point. Lucky to have been around him in my career - what a great guy he was. But did enough to get a chance to stay in the big leagues.

I was lucky that he hit my bat twice [in reference to a game on August 6th, when Terrell hit a pair of two-run homers off future Hall of Famer Ferguson Jenkins of the Chicago Cubs], would be the biggest thing that I could think of! One time, I was supposed to bunt, I thought it was a ball, so I pulled the bat back. Bobby Valentine's coaching third, and he didn't give me the bunt, so I gave him a, "Give me that sign again," and he didn't give anything, and I thought, "OK, I'll swing." So I'm thinking, "He's going to throw a strike because he knows I'm going to bunt," so I swung and hit it. And I tell everybody that the wind was blowing in 80 miles an hour, but I think it was blowing out 40, so I hit a home run. And then the second time, the same thing. I've played in some golf outings with Ferguson Jenkins, and he does remember - which shocks the hell out of me. I think he's lying to me. But a great day for Walt Terrell. And we won the game, 4-1, so a big day. I had 28 friends and family that were in the stands that day, so a wonderful time was had by all in Chicago later that evening.

MIKE FITZGERALD [Mets catcher from 1983-1984]: I remember getting called up with Clint Hurdle [in September], we did the flight together, and got to the ballpark in Philadelphia together. Charlie [Samuels] had new uniforms for us, new cleats, new everything. And I remember sitting at the locker, because we got there before the bus - we went straight to the ballpark. I remember seeing all my new gear and everything, and just thinking, "Well, I guess I made it, and I wonder if I'll get a chance to play while I'm up here." I was thinking to myself, *"I'd sure play me or give me a chance to play."*

But anyway, the bus got there, and I remember the first guy that came up and said "Hello" to me was George Foster. I don't know how George remembered my name - we were in spring training probably two years prior. Came up, said "Hello" to me, and asked me if I needed anything - bats, anything I wanted. So I used George's bat, my first at-bat [on September 13th], I believe it was the second inning, and was facing Tony Ghelfi - which I believe he as the Phillies' #1 pick in probably '79/'80, something like that. Threw a fastball, and hit it over the centerfield fence in Philly. I just remember running around the bases, kind of on air - running past Rose, Morgan, Schmidt, DeJesús - and thought, "You know what? I'm going to bring some life to this team. I'm going to bring some excitement. Somehow, someway, I'm going to help these guys start winning." That's what I told myself. It was a lot more difficult than that, but that was what I told myself when I got up there.

BRENT GAFF: I know my first win, Seaver started, and he went an inning [October 1st vs. the Expos at Shea Stadium, a game the Mets won, 5-4]. I think I got called up in September and I threw out of the pen. I don't know how I got a win [Gaff's 1983 record for the Mets was 1-0] - it must have been in relief. And then that winter, I played in Venezuela, and Bochy was my catcher. I was 8-1 there, with him behind the plate. That was the year we won the Triple A World Series, in '83. Gooden started and went seven and I closed the last two innings, and that was for the Triple A World Series Championship Game.

WALT TERRELL: We played pretty well in '83 - we came on and did some things. Some older guys went out and some younger guys came in, and we got to play. I think that was the biggest thing - we were better in '84 because we got to play a lot in '83.

CHAPTER 9:
THE TRADE THAT
TURNED IT ALL
AROUND

TIM McCARVER: I remember Frank Cashen calling me. I had an apartment the Mets got for me in Guttenberg, New Jersey. It was a great apartment in a bad area - near Fort Lee. I'd go over the George Washington every day. And Frank gave me a call on the 14th of June - at that time, the trading deadline was June 15th - and asked me about Keith Hernandez. He said, "I don't ask too many players or former players their opinions about things, but we've got a chance to get him relatively for a song. I want you to tell me the truth about what you know about Keith Hernandez." And I said, "He is about the best defensive first baseman I have ever seen." Not a guy who is going to hit for power, but I said, *"I'd get him in a heartbeat."*

RICK OWNBEY: I started at this point to get a little more comfortable with what was going on and a better understanding. When I ended up getting traded in that '83 season [Ownbey and Neil Allen were traded to the Cardinals for Hernandez], it was tough for me - even though Frank Cashen was in there and everybody, trying to make me clearly understand that they really did not want to trade me. But the Cardinals just wouldn't do the deal unless I was involved. But from my perspective, emotionally, I just didn't understand quite how "business" baseball is. If I knew what I know now, I would have looked at it completely different, because it felt like your family had said, "You're no longer part of the family," because I was so appreciative of the opportunity they had given me. And I'd worked really hard to try and do well for them. It's just part of the game and the business.

BOBBY VALENTINE: Neil was like one of our mainstays. He was ready to be some kind of dominating pitcher. And he was a fun-loving guy.

RICK OWNBEY: Complete surprise. It was the last day of the trade deadline. In fact, the way it went down, I was getting ready for the game. I'll never forget it - it was five minutes to 7:00, and I was in uniform and had one shoe on. I was tying it. And I can't remember who came to my locker and said, "Hey. They want to see you." I started to put my other shoe on, and they go, "No, no, no. They want to see you *right now.*" I was like, "Whoa. Did I do something wrong?" I had no idea. But when I opened the door and Frank and I can't remember who all were in there, you knew something was up.

I probably was one of the last to know, because I didn't know who to call - they told me I could call my family. I think I called my sister first, and she says, "Oh, we already know that. We saw it on ESPN." [Laughs] So I think she knew before me. Literally, came out of the office and had to take the uniform off, and if I'm not wrong, the next morning, flew out, and the colors change, the people. It was like starting all over. And I just wasn't really quite ready for it.

But it all did work out. The Cardinals are a tremendous organization, and because of the two for one, they didn't have room for me right then, so I did go back to the Triple A team. But lucky enough, Jim Fregosi was the manager at that time. Playing for Davey Johnson and Jim Fregosi - just tremendous. If you're a minor league ballplayer, any time I think you can play for a big league player and an ex-big league manager, it will make everyone on the team better.

STEVE ZABRISKIE: I will never forget the first night that Keith Hernandez walked on the field [June 17ᵗʰ, against the Montreal Expos at Olympic Stadium - a game the Mets would lose, 7-2]. And know this - I had known Keith since the early '70s. Keith and I were actually in the minor leagues together - at the beginning of his career and the end of mine. I had great respect for Mex [Henandez's nickname] as a person and as a player. He's the consummate professional. Regardless of what his personal life was like or what he might have done or might not have done with the Cardinals or whatever, not too many people on the Mets really cared. And I don't know how much of it was true, and I can't speak to that.

But it didn't matter, because when that guy walked on that infield the very first night that he was with the ballclub, the entire atmosphere - and I dare say it happened earlier, in the clubhouse, I know it did, because I was in there - and even attitude on that ballclub changed. Because the one thing that was really lacking was a leader. *And here's our leader.* Mex had never been the guy that had been the "rah rah/rally cry guy." He just went about it in such a professional way and let it be known that he didn't appreciate any half-efforts or any crap. Which is why he and Strawberry got into it once in spring training, because he led by example. He was a consummate professional and he carried himself that way, and he elevated that entire ballclub the very first night he walked on the infield. It was a critical component to what happened after that.

STEVE JACOBSON: It meant everything. He had the greatest effect on a team of anybody I've seen - other than Frank Robinson. I used to argue with Don Zimmer, "How can one guy make the other guys play better?" And Hernandez did. Hernandez made a better pitcher out of Dwight Gooden, and Gooden will give him credit for that. Wally Backman was a better second baseman. Hernandez elevated fielding to a high art. They talk about the great fielding first basemen of all time, and Hernandez was so good that the other teams couldn't bunt a runner from second to third. He would sprint, pick up the ball, and throw the runner out at third base.

He would go to Gooden and Bobby Ojeda...Ojeda, he would challenge. Ojeda came from the Red Sox [in 1986], where the pressures were a little different, and demand that Ojeda show him "balls." He would go to Gooden, and tell him, "This is what the hitter is trying to do in this situation. And this is what you have to try to make him do. *And this is how you do it.*" He would tell Backman that "A right hand hitter is looking to hit the ball to the right side of the infield. You have to play that." I can't say enough about what Hernandez meant to some young pitchers on that team - for courage and insight. He was very good.

GARY "BABA BOOEY" DELL'ABATE: It was almost like the reverse of the Seaver trade. It was like, "We got this really great player pretty easy. What's that all about?" And then you read later the whole drug thing in St. Louis and they had to unload him [Hernandez testified at a trial of a drug dealer in 1985, during which it was learned that he had used cocaine]. So that was kind of our good fortune. I liked him from the day he got there. I always refer to Keith Hernandez as he was like having an extra manager on the field. I remember watching those games even from the day he got there, and he would come off of first base and sort of yell to everyone. They would all look to him for direction. It was so awesome.

TOM GORMAN: I remember Keith getting to the Mets in '83, and he was kind of pissed about getting traded there, because obviously, of the history of us. But when he saw what young pitching the Mets had at the time, I think he got a little bit more excited about it. I remember him actually saying something in spring training of '84, that we were getting to the point where we had a pretty good core of young pitchers.

CRAIG SWAN: I played with Keith or against Keith in winter ball, and then we would see each other a lot, because back in the '70s, St. Louis and the Mets shared the same stadium in St. Pete, called Al Lang Field, for games. The thing about Keith is he was always kind of like a coach on the field. He was always coming in and saying something to the pitcher or saying something to the other infielders, or doing something to the outfielders and moving them around. He was like having a coach on the field, and that's what I remember. And a great team player, and a real nice guy. It was really nice to have Keith on the team. I felt bad for him in a way, because he had come from the Cardinals, who were a great team. But I think he and Whitey Herzog had a little disagreement, and that was it.

WALT TERRELL: It came as a surprise. I'm sure there were other trades that guys did really well, but I would say that it put some legitimacy to the Mets, so to speak. .300 hitter, great defensive player - he helped everybody in every phase of what was going on on the field. I know when I would be pitching, sometimes he would point his finger and say, "Hey, this guy is going," and I had hardly picked anybody off. So I throw to first, and pick somebody off - holy crap! Just his baseball intelligence and savvy made everybody better - immediately. It was an immediate deal. It wasn't, "It will take four or five months." Everybody was better *immediately.* The most significant thing that I remember - other than Dwight Gooden being on the '84 team. No doubt about it.

MIKE TORREZ: Keith was hyper - had always been hyper. I know when I was with the Cardinals earlier in my career [from 1967-1971], he was just coming up. But a great first baseman, and a lot of rah-rah chat. That's the kind of guys you needed to be successful - guys that would loosen up the guys, just bullshit with all the guys, and have fun. That's what Keith brought to the Mets. He was a hyper type character - Keith and I are still the best of friends. I really enjoyed playing with him. His defense was outstanding - nothing got by him. And it was great pitching, when left-handers came up, he'd make some terrific plays. And when we got in fights on the field, he was right there - he didn't back down. [Laughs]

TOM GORMAN: I thought Keith may have done more for our pitching staff than any pitcher that ever did anything for us - how's that? That pretty much sums him up, for me. You talk about a guy that knew hitters. I can recall him coming over, and Ken Oberkfell was one of his teammates from the Cardinals, and he ran over to me one time, and he said, "Why don't you just throw the ball in, and he'll hit a two-hopper to me." And sure enough, I threw a fastball in, and he hit a two-hopper to him, and Keith picked the ball up. Keith is one of those guys that could be playing first, but he could also be playing second - he could be so far off the bag sometimes that if a ball was hit to him, it would be a foot race to who was going to get to first, first.

But I thought he was really, really, really good about helping out the young guys. I think in '84, he realized he was on a team that has some really good young pitching, and that he might as well help them out with him being a veteran and knowing hitters. I can recall a game in Dodger Stadium, where I'm sitting in the dugout - it was right before the game. Steve Howe was pitching and Mike Scioscia was the catcher. Keith goes to me, "I'm going to get a base hit to right field on the first pitch when I'm up there." And I go, "Yeah Mex, right. Sure you are. How are you going to do that?" And he goes, "Well, I'm going to crowd the plate, and when the guy winds up to deliver, I'm going to step back, and I'm going to hit the ball into right field." And I said, "How do you know it's going to be a fastball?" And he says, "I'm not going to hit off of Howe. I'm going to hit off of *Scioscia.* Scioscia knows where I stand. I'm going to crowd the plate, he's going to think I've got a problem hitting the ball away, he's going to try and jam me."

Sure enough, the first pitch that Steve Howe throws…it wasn't Steve, it was another guy, a right hander - Keith hits a bullet into right field and he's running down to first base, and he kind of glances into the dugout, like, *"I told you so."* That was the kind of hitter he was. A total guess hitter. And he was always willing to help any of the young guys when it came to pitching to hitters. I always respected Keith for that, I really did.

JOHN STEARNS: Well, remember now, I was on the DL the whole year that year. So Keith came over, and obviously, we were in a rebuilding program, and he came in - that was probably the first step wasn't it, after the Seaver trade, to building a new [team]. He was obviously a really good player. Great defense and a really good hitter, so after we made that deal, everybody felt like the front office [was on the right track]. I think at that time, they solidified their position that they were going to rebuild and try to make the team a winner. I think the Wilpons showed their true feelings when they made that deal. And it was an excellent trade - he was the best first baseman in the game. He could hit, gave us a veteran influence over there, and it paid off with the '86 Series. That was a good deal for the Mets, because we didn't give up much and we got a great player. And obviously, he was a key part of the whole thing.

BOBBY VALENTINE: When you're living it, you don't do that judging [if Hernandez joining the Mets had an immediate effect on the team]. He was a really fun guy to be in the clubhouse and dugout with, and he was as energetic as anybody that I had ever seen in a uniform. I don't remember any major change that week or anything.

But I can tell you that it was really fun having him around. He was able to put the good part of the bat on the ball more often than I think anybody that we had at that time - for sure.

TIM McCARVER: He was the glue that held everything together with that team. His leadership on the field was insane. With runners on at first and second, and the way he covered the bunt play, it just enveloped the right side of the infield, and dared guys. The way to beat that play was to push it by him on the line - bunt it hard down the first base line. Normally, first basemen wouldn't want to do that. But with Hernandez, that's how you beat him. And he knew the opposition - really knew the opposition. And he took more chances.

RICK OWNBEY: I do, in some ways [think that if Ownbey remained with the Mets and not been part of the Hernandez trade, he would have had a better/longer career]. That's a tough one - it's hard to say. My comfort zone was starting to get good, and then when I got traded, it changed things. There's no doubt about it. And the Cardinal organization was definitely run different than the Met organization - not that either one was good, bad, or wasn't done correctly. But every organization is run a little different. For some reason - and maybe it was because I was drafted by them - I just felt really, really comfortable in the Mets organization. The one time I did meet Keith Hernandez, he was nothing but supportive and tried to make me understand what went on. He was obviously much more of a veteran and understood the business, where here I was this young player - involved in a trade that maybe I didn't want to be involved in.

PETE FALCONE: I remember Keith being so unhappy about being traded to the Mets from St. Louis. We were talking one night, he goes, "Pete, I'm a Met now." He was like, dejected. Three years later, *he was in the World Series.*

CHAPTER 10:
RECIPE FOR SUCCESS
(1984-1990)

STEVE ZABRISKIE: I think what really made the difference the next year was Davey Johnson, and of course, a couple of guys named Strawberry and Gooden. But I think Davey made a huge difference, because Davey's attitude…he didn't care what had happened before. He didn't care if the Mets had done horrible. He didn't care what had happened last week. He was just, *"This* is what we need to do to get better, and *this* is what we're going to do." Fortunately, he had Al Harazin, Joe McIlvane, and other people in the front office - not to mention Frank Cashen - who were committed to doing whatever it took to make that team better. And Frank had done it before in Baltimore. They had a plan. And to their credit, they stuck to their plan, and obviously, it paid off.

STEVE JACOBSON: Cashen brought Davey Johnson from the Orioles, essentially. And he had him managing at Triple A. He remembered Johnson was a questioner and a figure-it-out player with the Orioles. And also, a very good player. And brought Gooden up for the Triple A World Series. Gooden won the Triple A World Series for Johnson, and he was progressing so rapidly through the system. And Johnson recognized that, and had the nerve to use him, and brought him along. By the second year, Gooden was a world-beater [Gooden won the NL Cy Young Award in 1985, with a record of 24-4 and an ERA of 1.53]. Johnson eventually ran afoul of Cashen - that came several years later though.

TIM McCARVER: Things were catching. Darryl Strawberry came up in '83, the Keith Hernandez trade was made in '83, Dwight Gooden came up in '84, things started gelling, and the Mets were good. I mean, they were the talk of the town and walking very proudly in New York. *They were the toast of the town.*

BOBBY VALENTINE: It was a really wild group of guys that loved to be together. They loved to play baseball, they loved to compete amongst each other - as well as against the competition. If I had to be a smart guy or something, I can say I saw it coming. But I don't know that I saw it coming. I was always very positive, so I probably in 1984 was looking at the team, saying, "Wow. This is a team that could win." But I probably thought that in 1979 with the Mariners - I always thought that teams that I was around were going to win.

MIKE TORREZ: I knew they were going to be tough. They had some young players. See, a lot of those players enjoyed each other's company. When I was there, we all used to go out and go to dinner together and hung out together. And that's what Keith brought to the Mets. And Orosco, Darling, I remember all the guys would hang together and play together. That's why they were successful. Like I said, when you have that kind of togetherness on the team, good things happen. And that's what they wanted to happen, and they did.

BRENT GAFF: Those guys on the Triple A club stuck together, and all those veterans got moved out, and got a mindset in there, like, "We kicked everybody's ass before. *Why not do it again?"*

MIKE FITZGERALD: I think everybody thinks they're putting together a pretty good team. But I think the Mets at that point, with the guys that they had, as a group, they realized that it was their time. And sometimes that makes the difference. I can remember showing up to my second instructional league after my first full season in A ball, and I'm catching Tim Leary, Jesse Orosco, Mike Scott, Neil Allen, Jeff Reardon, and Brent Gaff. We had one of the best pitching staffs that I've ever caught that year, in I think it was the 1979 instructional league, in Florida. And I still have arguments with a couple of the Reds people about that, that they think their staff was better. But that was one of the staffs *I* ever caught.

WALT TERRELL: You could tell. I know the arms that they were accumulating at that point in the big leagues and at the Triple A level - the "younger arms," so to speak. And you've got Mookie Wilson and Wally Backman...and Hubie Brooks, who was absolutely tremendous. Pretty big deal guys. And I played with Kevin Mitchell in Triple A a little bit. There was talent in a lot of places, in a lot of positions, and there was obviously talent in the big leagues. A surprise? No. It was a matter of getting games in for the young guys and get to play.

And in 1984, we played very, very well - the Cubs just played better [the Mets finished in second place with a record of 90-72, 6.5 games behind the Cubs, who finished 96-65]. "Oh, you guys choked." We didn't choke, they just played better than we did, because we were up at one point, and they came into Shea Stadium and swept our butts [Walt may be referring to when the Cubs beat the Mets three games out of four at Shea from July 27th-29th, or when the Cubs swept the Mets four games at Wrigley Field from August 6th-8th]. I think Rick Sutcliffe was 16-1...are you kidding me? They just played better. Gary Matthews and those guys, they were just better than we were that year.

But we were for real that year - it wasn't a joke. Dwight Gooden, Lord have mercy - the most dominating game I've ever seen still to this day was his first game in the big leagues in Houston [on April 7th, when the Meats beat the Astros 3-2]. He struck out 16, and no disrespect to anybody that played on that team, but they had no chance. *Zero.* It was a mismatch, and he was 19 years old. Of all the games I've ever seen, that's the top pitching performance that I've ever seen, by far. And he wasn't that way all year - we all have our moments - but he had very few [bad outings].

TOM GORMAN: It was kind of one of those years [1984, when Gorman went 6-0 with the Mets], I could have gone 8-0. I always accuse Jesse of losing two of my games, but then he also saved a bunch of them, so I couldn't get on him too hard about it. But that was a really good year for me. More middle relief, come in, throw a couple of innings, the team scores a few runs, and you get the win - that kind of stuff. I think I may have started a game - I think I started against Pittsburgh and actually beat them. I think that was the one start I won, it could have been '84. But yeah, I won ten in a row with the Mets - if you add all three season. Seaver did it, but he did it all in '69. I did it '83, '84, and '85.

In '84, we win 90 games. In '85 we win 98 games. We just got [beat] by two hot teams - Chicago was hot that year with Sutcliffe and they had a great team, and then the following year, St. Louis had a really good team with Andújar, Tudor, and all that [the Mets finished in second place with a record of 98-64, 3 games behind the Cardinals, who finished 101-61]. 98 games should win you the division, and it just didn't. So you knew, sooner or later, they were going to do it - they just needed maybe a few more pieces. And they got them with a few acquisitions. The core of the team, the players were there, it was just a matter of could they put it together and beat one of those two teams. And obviously, they did in '86. I was released the last day of spring training in '86, and going into that spring training, I think everybody had the idea we were the team to beat in the National League East, really.

JOHN STEARNS: When you bring up two guys like Gooden and Strawberry, even though both turned out to be not as good as they probably should have been in their careers…I don't want to say that in a derogatory sense, because Gooden had a nice career, and Strawberry. Obviously, both those guys were as good as anybody in the game. I think that those two guys coming out of our farm system really changed things and set up the '86 championship season.

WALT TERRELL: I was traded for Howard Johnson, on December the 7th, 1984. Disappointed? Kinda, sorta. But it's baseball, and as long as I get to play, "where" was not always a concern. But I'd been there for a while, and was going to miss guys, but life goes on and we move on. After I got to Detroit, some guys said, "Yeah, it might have been best for HoJo to move on." So it worked out for both of us. I didn't win a World Series, but hell, a lot of people don't. Happy for him that it worked out good, and it worked out good for me - I stayed in Detroit a long time. I was very grateful to the people with the Mets, treated me very well. Hell, I'm not even sure I should have ever been in the damn big leagues! But they gave me an opportunity, and very fortunate to have ever played in the Mets organization.

JOHN STEARNS: And then, you go out and get Keith Hernandez and Gary Carter [on December 10th, the Mets acquired Carter in a trade with the Montreal Expos, for Hubie Brooks, Mike Fitzgerald, Herm Winningham, and Floyd Youmans]. That - along with Gooden and Strawberry - there was the core of your championship team right there.

MIKE FITZGERALD: When you're 23, you don't think, "What are they going to do with me now? Are they going to keep me?" The ironic thing about it was that morning, I had seen [Mets scout] Harry Minor's two sons, and said "Hi" to them briefly. They said, "How are you doing?", and I said,

"I'm doing great, and looking forward to next year." And they said, "Well, dad just got home from the winter meetings, and it looks like they're going to give you a chance to play." And then that afternoon, I got a phone call, and was traded.

JEFF REARDON: I respect Gary Carter a lot as a catcher. When Montreal got rid of him, I was thinking, *"That could be the final piece to the puzzle, right there."* Because he knew how to call a game and he was a gamer. Yeah, some people got on him being into himself. Well, he was like a little kid - he wanted to win all the time. He hated losing. To me, he was a team player. I think the "selfish" things you hear about him, that's jealousy coming from other people. Because you couldn't have met a nicer guy who played the game.

CRAIG SWAN: Especially when they got Gary - Gary and Keith really I think were the biggest two reasons. And Doc was throwing well, and Strawberry was coming into his heyday. And they had those scrappy guys - Lenny Dykstra and Backman. Those guys were great at getting on base and moving people over, and then they had Keith and Gary right behind them. It turned into a good team, and then they got some good pitching - they got Darling, and Sid Fernandez was a real pitcher then. They had some quality starters. It was kind of the way the Mets won back in '69 and '73 - they had three real good starters. It was a similar team.

TIM McCARVER: I could see it coming. It was easy. If you are a baseball fan, if you're any judge of talent, when you see a 20-year-old Dwight Gooden do what he did in 1985...I had the pleasure of catching - I don't know if "pleasure" is the proper word - but I caught Bob Gibson for all those years. And then in 1968, he had that remarkable year [Gibson won the NL Cy Young Award, with a record of 22-9 and an ERA of 1.12]. I put Gooden's year as the second best year I ever saw in 1985, when he was 24-4, with an earned run average of 1.53. *Phenomenal.* So, it's pretty easy to put your cart behind those horses. I mean, with Strawberry and Hernandez, and they picked up Ray Knight [who was traded to the Mets on August 28, 1984, in exchange for players to be named later, which turned out to be Gerald Young, Manuel Lee, and Mitch Cook], and Frank Cashen put that organization together - really wound it tightly together.

CRAIG SWAN: I got released [on May 9, 1984]. Davey was the manager. When you get released, it's not too much fun. The one thing I remember about getting released, we were leaving that night for California, and Davey, because he was such an avid golfer, would let players bring their golf clubs on trips. Because we didn't play [baseball games] until 7:00 at night all the time. I remember carrying my clubs in, and then I got the call from Davey, and said, "You're released." I was pretty upset. I had to go get my clubs and take them back to the car and drive out of the stadium. I think I cried all the way home, I was so upset.

It was the only team I had ever been with, really. I signed with them and knew everybody in the front office. It was an upsetting day, but you get over it. There's not much you can do when your arm is bad. I knew things were not good for me, because I could feel things going on in my arm that weren't good. It didn't really hurt that much, it would get really tired real fast, and then I had some tingling coming down from my tricep area into my fingers, and that wasn't normal. I could throw the ball about 90 miles an hour for about 40 pitches, and then after that, it was down to 80 miles an hour. I knew something was wrong, and it was upsetting that my arm went when it did. But that's the way it goes. Ernie Banks, he never played on a winner, either. You can't get upset by that - it's just all timing.

JOHN STEARNS: I tried to play in '85, I still couldn't play. I actually went down and played for my hometown team, the Denver Zephyrs' Triple A team - I'm from Denver. I tried to play there, I didn't catch, I played first base. And I watched the Mets. I had to watch them all through that '86 season and it was tough not being there, having put in ten years of hard work there, and then I missed out on that whole '86 thing. I watched it, and I had to go through that whole thing. And by then, of course the Carter trade had happened and I was completely out of the picture, but I had to watch the '86 Series from a bar. And I had to bite my lip. It was tough missing that whole thing. It was all part of the injury thing for me - the elbow - that I couldn't play anymore. I don't know what would have happened had I still been playing. I don't know if I would have been traded or not.

RANDY JONES: The other side of the coin too, remember my former team, the Padres, made it to the World Series in '84. The years after I retired, I got frustrated - both teams were in the World Series in just a couple of years. I'm going, "What the hell? Why me, man? *Come on!"*

JERRY KOOSMAN: I still followed them, and was happy for them - that they were getting stronger and stronger. Of course, Jesse Orosco, I have to give him a plug - we were traded for each other. So I followed Jesse and I was happy for what he did for the Mets, too. But certainly, Ron Darling and Sid Fernandez - there was a bunch of good talent that came along.

JEFF REARDON: There are a lot of guys on that ['86] team that I came up with, so I was rooting for them all the way. I'm still a Met fan. People ask me, "Who do you root for." I say, "I root for the Mets and the Red Sox." That's who I rooted for growing up, because I'm from Massachusetts - I've got Boston on this side of me and the other side I've got the Mets. So those are my two teams, and luckily, I got to play for both of them. I was rooting for the Mets [in the 1986 World Series, despite both teams being Reardon's favorites]. I was personal friends with Gary, and I didn't know any of the Red Sox guys. I actually was rooting for the Mets. And Jesse Orosco, I was very excited for him - when he threw up his glove [after striking out the final batter]. I said, "Oh boy, I hope I get the chance to do that." Wouldn't you know, the next year I did [when the Minnesota Twins beat the Cardinals in the World Series], but I didn't get a strikeout. I would have probably done the same thing - thrown the glove up in the air. But I got them out one, two, three, so I guess it doesn't matter.

I think that, also [that if the Mets didn't trade Reardon, they may have made the playoffs in '84, '85, and '87]. I also think if I stayed in New York for many years, I would be in the Hall of Fame. I mean, I've beaten all the guys in the Hall of Fame with saves, but they try and go on this thing about I came up in a different era. Well, why was Goose Gossage and Bruce Sutter and all of them playing at the same time as me? They try to classify me as a "one inning closer" - that wasn't until I got to the Red Sox [in 1990, Reardon's twelfth season], and I was still more than a one inning closer. One-inning closers, I think Dennis Eckersley is who started that. So I always felt that I got a little screwed on the Hall of Fame thing, because I had to go to cities like Montreal, Minnesota - not big towns. I mean, when I went to Boston, yeah, I broke the record in '92 [when he topped Rollie Fingers' mark of 342 saves - and finished his career with 367], and the first thing they're saying is, "Automatic first ballot." *I didn't even make the ballot.* So I felt like I really got screwed and there's nothing I can do, because I've lost out on the old-timers' committee too, just last year [2014]. I'm not real happy, but I know I'm one of the best closers - I don't care what they say.

STEVE JACOBSON: You could see it coming. And the Cardinals resented that the Mets got so much ink. They didn't understand - this was in USA Today, and [someone from the Cardinals] said, "How come the Mets make the lead story when we're in first place?" Well, because the Mets game was over an hour earlier, and newspaper deadlines are what they are. I just remember going into the Cardinal clubhouse and they were bitching about the Mets getting more coverage! In '86, the Mets were establishing themselves, and the Cardinals were defending champions, and the Mets went to St. Louis and Whitey Herzog changed his pitching rotation for the Mets. And the Mets beat him, and the last game of the series was a day game, and Darling beat the Cardinals. Herzog was lamenting his change in pitching, which didn't get him anything. And the last line of my piece that day was, "The Mets left Herzog a sadder *Budweiser* man."

TOM GORMAN: We played hard and we partied hard - I'm not bringing up the drug end of it, because it wasn't that way when I was there, to be honest with you. But we went out to bars and stuff like that - we had a good time doing that. But we'd sit in the back of the plane and play cards. Everybody...let's say the Rustys and the other guys on the team, I think they may have given us that nickname, "The Scum Bunch." But it was Jesse, myself, Doug Sisk, Brent, Danny Heep - just guys that hung together. And when the game was over in St. Louis, we'd all go out to a bar and have a few drinks. It was kind of a group that we hung with. We'd go fishing together, we'd do all sorts of stuff. I don't even know who gave us the name, the Scum Bunch, but that was our nickname. I don't know if we were proud of it, but we accepted it! [Laughs]

I'll tell ya, this will be a good book, because if you talk to the right people...this could be an entertaining book! Because there were some characters on that whole stretch from when I showed up, all the way through '89. Some people would argue that it would be me [who was the biggest "character" on the Mets]. I think between Roger McDowell, Jesse, and myself, and Scotty Holman and that group. I mean, we used to do some stuff, like Vern Hoscheit was our bullpen guy. Vern always had to have the control of the bullpen, so we would just screw with him - we'd lock him out of the bullpen, or we'd put eye black and Vaseline on the phone, and then have Mel Stottlemyre call us up, and I'd say, "I'll get it," and Vern would say, *"I answer the phone around here!"* So he grabbed the phone, puts it up to his ear, and there's Vaseline dripping off his chin and eye black all over his ear!

I got kicked out of the bullpen twice. How do you kick a reliever out of the bullpen? He called up Davey, and said, "Get Fax out of here! *I've had enough!"* I get on the phone and Davey goes, "Come on down to the dugout." I go down to the dugout, I'd sit down there, and it would be like, the sixth inning, and he'd say, "You'd better get back to the bullpen, I'm going to be needing you!" It's funny, I got kicked out of the bullpen twice, and both times I pitched that game - one time in St. Louis and one time there. So those are the kind of things that I remember. But Roger was probably the biggest character on the whole club. I mean, the 'Seinfeld' episode where he's spitting on Kramer is a perfect example, because he'd be that guy to do that!

TIM McCARVER: Obviously, it topped off with that Game 6 of the playoffs against Houston [in 1986, which the Mets won in 15 innings, 7-6, to advance to the World Series], and then of course, the World Series. How the Mets won it that year, they could very well have just been a Division Champion, and not a World Series Champion. It's hard to believe they won 108 games in the season and could very easily have lost to Houston, and if they got to Game 7, they'd have to face Mike Scott [who won the NL Cy Young Award that year, and was voted NLCS MVP - despite the Astros losing the series]. And then of course, Roger

Clemens coming out in Game 6 in the World Series [which the Mets would win in dramatic fashion, and go on to win the deciding Game 7 and the World Series].

STEVE JACOBSON: I think there was eight years in a row where the Mets outdrew the Yankees. It may have been six, but I have the idea that there was a long string of when the Yankees were not very much, and the Mets were good. The Mets should have won again in '87 and '88. But didn't.

TIM McCARVER: The surprising thing is that they didn't win more often than they did.

STEVE ZABRISKIE: '88 and '89 were huge disappointments, because we just expected to be there. Y'know, "We're going to win the whole thing." And when it didn't happen, it was like, *"What happened?"* And I'm sure fans felt the same way. It was like, "That isn't supposed to happen." Because the team was really that good, and they believed in themselves to that degree.

CHAPTER 11: REASONS FOR THE DOLDRUMS (1977-1983)

JOHN STEARNS: I think obviously the ownership group was a little slow coming around to the fact that…they were used to paying players…when I got to the big leagues in '75, the players were making nothing. I mean *nothing.* I'm talking the big league minimum was $15,000. And you had to have five good years to make $50,000. And hardly anybody was making $100,000 - that was "the top figure." $100,000 was a big deal. Seaver made $100,000, after about eight, nine, or ten years of excellence. What was happening was the owners had a completely different mindset - they were taking all the money. I mean *all* of the money. Millions. And paying the players nothing. It took the Player's Union to come around, and Curt Flood won the free agency thing [the famous "Seitz decision" on December 23, 1975], that changed everything.

But even in '77, I believe Tom Seaver was only making $100,000 a year. It's hard to believe when you think about today. And even in the last 30 years, you don't even have to be a star - if you're just an every day player today, an average Major League player, you're making five million dollars. The Mets' front office, Donald Grant and the Paysons were old school people that treated the players awful when it came to money. They were nickel and diming you over $5,000 and $10,000. It was *old school.* It was like when you go back to the '30s, '40s, and '50s, when the players didn't make anything - you had to have a job in the off-season. And I know they were raking in *millions* of dollars - from TV income, from income at the stadium. I don't know what the players' payroll was in 1975 through 1977, but it was hardly anything [the average players' salary in 1975 was $44,676, in 1976 was $51,501, and in 1977 was $76,066]. Wasn't it just like, two or three million for the entire team?

I made $15,000 in 1975, as a rookie for the Mets. I was there all year, and I made *$15,000.* So getting back to the front office, yes, I do think the Mets, their owners were old school and they were slow coming around to the new rules and regulations of the game - which included free agency. Instead of going out and spending some money, I think they were worried about making their several whatever they were making, which had to be millions. They didn't want to cut back on that. And that's why they got rid of Seaver. "He's making $100,000. Let's get rid of him. We've got to get into a rebuilding program."

Today, do you know what the rookie minimum is? It's $500,000. So I think the owners for the Mets were slower coming around and adjusting, and then the free agency thing happened, and people started giving players bigger contracts. And while I was still there, the money jumped up from everybody making under $100,000 to...I actually signed a five-year contract for $1.8 million, which is $300, $300, $400, $400, $400, in a five-year span. Which was ridiculously high at that time back then. But that's how quickly everything jumped up after Curt Flood had somehow got that ruling to be a free agent. And that changed everything. It's gone up huge from there.

CRAIG SWAN: Absolutely, 100% [the fact that the Mets didn't sign big name free agents during the late '70s was the major reason for their lack of success]. There's no doubt in my mind.

JERRY KOOSMAN: Don Grant was a pretty conservative "main voice" of the Mets. So they didn't go out and spend too much money. And I don't remember just which year he was not playing an active role anymore. [Grant was fired at the end of the 1978 season]

CRAIG SWAN: When Doubleday and Wilpon bought the team, that's kind of when it shifted. What happened early, when free agency was created in '76, the Mets' existing owners and general manager and president, M. Donald Grant, they did not want to get involved with free agency. They were very upset that free agency was established, so they totally stayed away from it, and really never involved themselves in it. The Mets didn't get free agents until Doubleday and Wilpon bought it.

STEVE JACOBSON: Yankee games were full of excitement, and there were [Met] games when the chant of "LET'S GO METS!" became "LET'S GO HOME!" Steinbrenner's concept of having a star like staffing a Broadway production was quite evident, when he negotiated for Reggie Jackson as a free agent [for the 1977 season], and the Mets wouldn't keep pace. Certainly, the revenue potential for the Mets was not as good as the Yankees, but damn near. They still had New York. And a lot of people felt that New York was still a "National League city."

PETE FALCONE: It was just a tough time for the whole organization. Even in the minor leagues, even in spring training...see, I came from the Cardinals. And the Cardinals had more of an "excitement" in spring training. We had good teams - we had the potential to maybe win and be in first place, if things clicked. The New York Mets, we just went to spring training, "Hey, we're playing this year - let's see if we can finish in fourth place." That's the way it was.

JOHN STEARNS: It didn't affect me at all, because I just tried to play harder. But I played hard anyway, so I would have played exactly the same with a winning team as I did then. I tried to come in and give my 120%, and play for the team. That's the thing. *You've got to play for the team.* You've got a man on second base, you try to get him over with less than two outs. If it's less than one out, you try and get the guy over to third. I would give up an at bat and try to hit a grounder to second base. The other players on the team knew that. We didn't really have a veteran leader at that time, but I think they saw what I was trying to do. So when you're losing, I just tried to come out and play as hard as I could every day. Play a team game, and show my teammates how we could play and win. That's what I tried to do.

My approach to sports - and I played college football, and I'm not saying this is for everybody, and I'm not saying it's right - was "There's the other team, they're trying to beat me up, so I'm going to try and beat them up, because if I don't, I'm going to get beat up." So that's how I approached sports. I didn't want to be friends with the opponent, I didn't want to talk to them during the game, I didn't want to be "buddy-buddy" with them - especially during the game. I just didn't do that. I never talked to any of the opposing players while the game was going on.

And I tried to play as hard as I could every day. I was *mad* playing - obviously, because we were losing a lot. So by losing, going 60-90 every year, it's frustrating, and I was pissed all the time. I just played as hard as I could and I played strictly for the team - I did everything that I could for the team. And I'm sure the other players didn't like me. I think some of my own teammates, I was a little too brash for them. But if you look at it, if you're an owner running the team or a manager, you want a guy like me, because I'm out there playing hard, trying to win every day. So that's the approach I took - I wanted to win, I was pissed that we were losing, and I played mad and hard.

PETE FALCONE: There were a lot of bright spots, we just couldn't put it together. Yeah, we'd win two or three in a row, but then we would lose ten games in a row. [Laughs] I remember sometimes going to the west coast, and back then, you'd get these west coast swings - first you went to LA, then you went to San Diego, then you went to San Francisco, and on the way back, you'd stop at Pittsburgh and St. Louis. I think a few times we went to the west coast, didn't even win *a game* out there. Maybe pulled out a couple of games coming home in St. Louis or in Pittsburgh, and that was it - "We're back!"

STEVE JACOBSON: Bob Bailor told me that the players had no relationship with each other. This was earlier in the '80s. And they were like, playing cards and picking out this card, and one card didn't have any relationship to the cards you already had in your hand. It was a disjointed team.

DAN NORMAN: We had some young pitchers coming up - some great pitchers, that could have really turned the Mets around. We had Jeff Reardon, Mike Scott, Neil Allen, Jesse Orosco, Ed Lynch, Juan Berenguer, John Pacella - all those guys were coming up to fill a void and fill the need that the Mets needed. But if you look later on, those guys ended up getting traded. Reardon ended with three hundred and something saves [367] - he had the record for years, once he went to the Expos. You had Mike Scott, who did excellent. Jesse Orosco was part of that World Series. Neil Allen was traded, Juan Berenguer, Roy Lee Jackson was traded. That's a pretty good pitching staff, if you look at it, after what they did with their careers after they let the Mets.

PAT ZACHRY: It was just one or two hitters, one or two pitchers, and the whole thing is completely different. Apparently, they finally got rid of enough of us and had enough nucleus of their younger guys later on that came up, and that's all it took. It's what they needed. And bless their hearts - the fans stuck with them. And they finally got rid of that guy waving the cards around back there and got some people that were really interested in baseball!

CRAIG SWAN: That's one thing that baseball is good about - it seems to connect family members. I think it was something I didn't realize when I played, but after I got done, I realized that by being a baseball player, I was something that people could talk about, could converse about, and could connect to other people about. I got that a few years after I played. I didn't get that when I was playing - it was too much pressure.

CHAPTER 12:
TORRE

SKIP LOCKWOOD: I thought Joe was a special guy. He came from being a player, and many managers do that, also, but I thought Joe had a special insight. It's hard to lay your finger on exactly what he did differently, but the one thing I would say that Joe got to know each individual - about him and their family. So he would be the kind of guy that would know you much more intimately, I guess, than any other managers were. It wasn't necessarily that he just knew you on the field - he would know your family situation, he would know if your mother was having a birthday. Joe was the kind of guy that would come to find you before the game, and talk about what was going on. Joe didn't sit around in the bullpen or in the dugout when the practice was going on - Joe was much more "on the field." He's very knowledgeable about the game, but he was also very knowledgeable about people.

LENNY RANDLE: Everybody was loose - there was no uptightness. We played hard, had a lot of fun, and tried to win. And Torre was building a little empire - he was building a little future Yankee-type/Dodger-type team, that I guess they didn't have patience with. But he was a phenomenal brain.

STEVE HENDERSON: All I know about Joe is he really took care of me. When I first got there, he called me in his office and he talked to me about having fun and playing the game, and just enjoying myself while I was up there. He eased me into the line-up - he didn't rush me into the line-up. It helped me out a lot, because dealing with the media, he took care of me.

PAT ZACHRY: For what we had, he did as best as he could. I don't know of anybody else in the game that can garner more respect than Joe. Just a super person. It's a shame that we never did give him the kind of team he probably deserved. But it was good to see him do well with the Yankees [Torre would win four World Series as the Yankees' manager - 1996, 1998, 1999, and 2000 - the latter against the Bobby Valentine-managed Mets, and would be inducted into the Baseball Hall of Fame in 2014]. I was glad to see all that happen and transpire. It's a shame it didn't occur as a Met, but you don't come up to the big leagues and start hitting .300 right away. Most people don't. It takes a while to learn everything - and I suppose that's the way it was for him as a manager.

STEVE JACOBSON: Torre obviously became a very good manager. If he had stayed long enough, he might have matured much earlier than he did, and his influence on the team might have been very good. He was a very good player. As a player, he was very strong on the union. He became a spokesman for all of the other players on the Cardinals, to the point where McCarver told him, "You can't handle everybody's problems and remain as good as you are." One of the favorite lines of Torre's concept of managing was that he hit .360 and .240, and he said, *"I tried every bit as hard."* He understood that, and owners and managers don't always often understand that.

LENNY RANDLE: Torre would tell me, "You've got to be a psychologist at third and talk to the pitchers like a catcher, to make them feel like they're never alone. You've got to say things to keep them relaxed. You've got to be funny, you've got to get their mind off the game and back into the game. You've got to talk about their kids' shoes, going to school, what you ate." He'd give me all these scenarios, and he actually did it - and it worked!

So, when he came out to the mound, it wasn't like always, "What are you going to throw this guy? Pitch him up and in," and all this serious stuff. It was, "We're OK here. You've got a 3-2 count. You've got your 75 or 80 pitches in. I can take you out, but I'm thinking you want to get out, or do you want to stay in and tough it out?" He was checking the character of the guy. If he had guts enough or was tired or partied all night, he could tell. Because he was a catcher and player/manager, and was phenomenal at reading people and personalities. We had a great time with his tutelage.

JEFF REARDON: I enjoyed playing for him. I was a huge baseball fan of all the teams growing up, and I know how many good years he had. He was nice to me, and gave me that shot. He did call me up and he used me a lot. Very friendly guy. But he wanted 100%. He wanted you hustling and no slacking off. He was a good manager. I felt bad for him all the years he didn't have a job. I used to see him at golf tournaments and after he went to Atlanta - I'd talk to him, and he'd say, "I can't get a job." Then to find out he takes the Yankees, and look what he did with them.

GARY "BABA BOOEY" DELL'ABATE: I almost have zero recollection of him as a manager of the late '70s and early '80s. If Torre didn't manage the Yankees to all those championships, he'd have just been "another guy in the parade." Which he sort of was, anyway. I remember him more as a player, and again, my dad would fill in the blanks - "He was a legend when he played in St. Louis." But I don't really remember him managing that much.

STEVE JACOBSON: Players [was the difference between Torre enjoying great success as a manager of the Yankees, compared to his tenure with the Mets]. Torre was recognized himself that he had an "adult team," and he managed them as adults. He had no use for...who was the guy that they called "The Village Idiot" in Texas? [Rubén Sierra] The outfielder that had been around for several years, but did not understand that winning was the point, not your statistics. And the pitcher that wore Babe Ruth's hat [David Wells], but I do remember that Torre was very uncomfortable with him, but he knew how to keep their distance and employ the pitcher, who was actually quite effective, and an important force in Torre's winning. Torre was just an adult who treated his players as adults, recognized what Derek Jeter had. And when they picked up players, look at the early Yankee success under Torre, when they had Tim Raines, Darryl Strawberry, and Chili Davis as "role players." And they were marvelous additions. Paul O'Neill thrived under Torre.

LENNY RANDLE: Joe Torre was a combination of Dr. Phil, he had some Billy Martin in him, he was an ambassador, he was very diplomatic, and he could be very sarcastic. He could be like Billy Crystal, and then he could turn around and be like, the Hulk. [Laughs]. You could read his face if he was pissed off, and you didn't want to piss him off, because he was always polite - he didn't have to say much, he just had a look, a presence, and an aura, that you respected him...and his brother, Frank, who would come around quite around, and his buddy, Tim McCarver.

All these Cardinal guys would come around - the shortstop that ended up being our coach, Dal Maxvill. He was around some winning guys that won World Series, and we respected that. Bob Gibson would drop in, and go, "Hey Joe." Like...*whoa!* Here's his buddies. And Lou Brock, who was still playing, and Joe was still younger than Lou Brock, and yet he was managing, goes, "Lenny, go spend some time with Lou. He'll pay the fine if they catch you." [Laughs] He was just that kind of guy. He wanted you to get the best out of yourself and learn from the best in the business. So he was a great manager and a great personality.

CHARLIE PULEO: I only knew him the time he came down to Tidewater. He'd just say "Hello" and "Good luck." And then in New York, those guys are out of the old school. They'd make you earn your way - him and Gibson both didn't really talk a lot to the rookies. Like I said, they didn't talk to me until I started that ballgame. And that's just the way it was back then. You had to earn your way. I didn't think twice of it. And I didn't really know much of what went on that year, except the time I was there.

DAN NORMAN: There were a lot of comments from the other players that he needed more experience at that time. I'm sure he did - I don't know, I never managed. I thought we could have won more ballgames. It just didn't happen. We lost some close games. And as you know, he became a very great manager. I just wanted to play and show what I could do.

LENNY RANDLE: I can remember vividly Torre was trying to get us to loosen up more. Have more fun. Play hard and have fun, because you play better when you relax. He would go out to the mound for example, and say, "Hey Tom," and [Seaver] would say, "I'm not leaving. I'm not getting out of here." And Joe would go, "OK. I want you to loosen up though." He goes, "Joe, I'm loose." "Well, where did you go last night?" "I went to Mamma Leone's last night." "What did you eat?" "I ate tagliatelle and pasta pescatore...and I think I have gas." And he would fart on the mound! So that loosened everybody up - Buddy would go, "Whatever you do, don't hit them to me!" And then Tom says, "I'm getting out of here - I'll get this guy out, and then you can take me out, Joe. But right now, *that fart is hanging over the mound.*" He struck the next guy out, left the game, and we were so glad. I could hear Ralph Kiner or Bob

Murphy going, "I wonder what they're saying on the mound? It must be some serious strategy going on." Little did they know...

CHAPTER 13:
MAYS & GIBSON

RANDY JONES: Joe Torre was a player's type manager, and surrounded himself with good guys - Willie Mays would be around the clubhouse [and served as a coach from 1974-1979], and having Bob Gibson as the pitching coach [in 1981]. Veteran guys who knew how to win, and knew what it took to win.

STEVE HENDERSON: That same year [that Henderson joined the Mets], we had a coach by the name of Mr. Willie Mays. He helped me out a lot.

PAT ZACHRY: There's not a bigger ballplayer - name or player-wise or anything else - at that time, maybe a guy like Mickey Mantle, or maybe a Hank Aaron - but there just weren't any bigger names than someone like Willie Mays. And was so approachable. Such a good every day type person. Even our minor league guys that he was exposed with, they just loved him. Everybody loved him. And he was so easy to get along with, such a good-natured person. Not at all like some of the other major league guys that you saw.

Always accessible, Willie was. Would do anything for you if he thought he could help you. And didn't ever ask a dime. He was just one of those guys that would take care of everybody. If Willie was down to his last penny, he'd give it up to make sure somebody had something. That's just the kind of guy he is. I stayed at his house - my wife and I did - in '78. Never charged me a penny, just "Take care of a few of the bills on it - if you run the air conditioner, pay the electric bill." Just a wonderful man, truly a wonderful man.

STEVE HENDERSON: He helped me get a car, he took care of me - tried to help me the best way he can. And when you're there, you're playing away and people try to compare you - there ain't no way I was going to be compared to Willie Mays. There is only one Willie Mays. I have a lot of respect for that guy.

DAN NORMAN: One time, I thought I should have made the team. I was in spring training, and I led the team in everything - offensively. I thought that's what you're supposed to do to make the team. But the last day, they sent me to Triple A. So they thought I was going to make some bad comments about the Mets, but that's not my nature and wasn't my character. But they sent Willie Mays to talk to me. So they called him from California at the time, and he came out to Virginia, and stayed about three days, talking to me. He said he didn't think it was my character either - to badmouth the organization. Which I never did. I thought they just made their decision, and I just had to go keep playing until I got called back up.

   But a good guy - helped me with outfield work and with hitting. But there was a problem too at the time - he was working with a casino. He and Mickey Mantle. So they couldn't work with the casino *and* be in baseball. The commissioner made them make a choice [in 1979 - the same year he was inducting into the Baseball Hall of Fame - Mays was forced to quit as the Mets' hitting instructor after becoming a "goodwill ambassador" for the Bally's Park Place hotel and casino in Atlantic City, resulting in a ban from Major League Baseball until 1985]. I'm glad I got the chance to meet him in my baseball career, because I used to watch him play all the time.

JERRY KOOSMAN: Willie, just having him around meant a lot. Willie had so many instincts he played by, and maybe some of them were hard to teach. But if you watched him, you learned a lot. But Willie was a good baseball man and fun to talk to. And he did have a lot he could teach, too. You've got an all-time Hall of Famer there, that's fun to have on your side.

BOBBY VALENTINE: I remember sometime in either '77 or '78, where Lee Mazzilli had the "basket catch," and there may have been only three guys who ever played centerfield who tried to use that basket catch. Of course, Willie I think was the first. And I remember Willie working with Maz. But he was working with the good players - he never really worked with me. And he was always a super guy.

JOHN STEARNS: He didn't really have a large coaching role, but was a good guy. He was hanging out and in the locker room and suiting up and getting out for pre-game. Just a good guy to have around the team. Willie Mays, of course, was one of the top five baseball players in history, with Babe Ruth, Hank Aaron, Lou Gehrig, and Ty Cobb. That was a thrill to have him around.

RANDY JONES: I remember when I first got to spring training, my first spring training down in Florida, I got to St. Petersburg, and I had a nice long talk with Gibby. And Gibby being a power type pitcher, the way he pitched, he knew that I was a sinker ball/slider pitcher. He looked at me, and said, "Why don't I just give you the ball every fifth day?" And I said, "That's a great idea, Gibby!" That's basically what it was all about. I'm 31 years old, I've already been around for eight years in the big leagues. I just loved the guy - as far as his mental approach and stuff, we pretty much agreed and saw eye to eye. I thought he did a good job with what he had, but sometimes, it's pretty hard. The mental part of the game, I thought Gibby did a great job on. As far as the mechanics and the fundamentals and stuff, it was pretty tough for him to take what he knew and what he had success with and transfer it to some of the guys.

JEFF REARDON: Gibby was a pretty tough pitching coach. He taught you to be tough. He'd tell you to go knock someone on their ass. And you'd better do it, or he'd give it to you in the dugout when you came in. I don't think the taught too much more to the bullpen - it seemed like he worked with the starters more, probably because he was a starter, he had the same mindset. And there was somebody else helping the relievers. He did help, but I think his thing was the starters, because he was so good as a starter.

PAT ZACHRY: He would try and get you to toughen up and throw certain pitches, and try to teach you as much as he could. A very good pitching coach.

CHARLIE PULEO: He was there when I went up. He was a good guy. Like I said, those guys are just "old school." But gosh almighty, the careers they had, they deserve to have it any way they want to. We talked when I was out there pitching. We did talk a bit about pitching in ballgames. I wasn't there that much - we were in the playoffs in Tidewater that year, and I might have been up there for three weeks or so. I guess they liked what I did, because they were happy with what I did in that start I had. I didn't know if they thought they were going to be fired. It sounded like they thought they were coming back. But I guess you never know.

PETE FALCONE: Gibby came from a different era, and he couldn't do much with us. I remember he tried here and there. He tried to toughen people up - I don't know what he was trying to do, what the Mets were thinking about. Gibby was not the answer for that team. Nothing against Gibby - great career, great Hall of Famer. But no, we had just too many young pitchers who really didn't have their own identity yet. And they weren't really established as bona fide major leaguers. I mean, we had some good guys that threw great, like Jeff Reardon and Mike Scott and Pat Zachry and

Swanie.

But we didn't have the consistency. We didn't gel. There was no real mentor, see? There was nobody to look up to. And that was one of the problems of that team - there was no Tom Seaver to look up to. Or a Jerry Koosman or a Nolan Ryan. That was the thing that was missing - there was no leadership on that team. It was like a bunch of guys walking around with no real identity. We just had a uniform, we're playing baseball - "Let's try to win a game here."

CHAPTER 14: BAMBERGER

JOHN STEARNS: George was a good old guy. He was a great guy to play for. He never raised his temper up at all. I think Frank Cashen [recommended Bamberger] because he was the pitching coach for the Orioles - I'm not sure about that. But he didn't have a lot of managerial experience. He didn't have a lot to work with, and he was only here for about a year and a half. Was he the right choice? Who knows? We weren't ready to win at that time yet. And I don't know if anybody could have done any better job than that. He took over for Torre, and then Torre in his later years got some talent and showed that he was a great manager. But Bamberger, good guy, great guy, loved playing for him. He was managing a National League game, which is not easy - you have to double-switch and things like that. I thought he did a decent job, but we didn't have enough to win yet.

CRAIG SWAN: For me, Bambie was great, because I was just starting to rehab my arm then, and I went back down to instructional league after that '81 season. And Bambie was there at the Mets complex. He must have known he was going to get the job - I don't exactly know when he was hired [October 20, 1981], but he started me throwing. And he came out, and I think Bambie was the first one I started playing catch with, and over weeks and months, we started ten feet away, and then maybe the next day, went to fifteen feet. He started out so slow - it really rehabbed my arm in a slow way, that I think really was part of me coming back and winning eleven games that year. I remember him as a very gentle coach, who kind of knew how to rehab an arm.

He was a pitching coach prior to being a manager, so he knew his stuff there. And really a nice, nice man. Just a very sweet man.

RANDY JONES: I loved George Bamberger. Once again, a player's manager, and a lot of energy he brought. And having a pitching background, I was excited to have him as my manager, and I wasn't disappointed about what he did, as well. I mean, I thought George was great. Once again, that might have been the start of it right then and there - if you look at that team, a lot of the same guys from the year before, but overall, it was a decent season. Once again, pitching, Craig Swan had a positive year, Mike Scott had the potential that we saw later on in his career with Houston, and Jesse Orosco was still getting his feet wet. Some good names. Once again, day in and day out, there wasn't this kind of line-up that you needed on a consistent basis to win, I don't think.

CHARLIE PULEO: George was a great guy. Easygoing. As a pitcher, he liked to see you work out of situations that a lot of people would just take you right out of the ballgame. He gave a pitcher a lot of confidence, because he gave you a chance to show that you could get out of something and stay in the ballgame. I pitched more than I think I ever pitched that many innings in the big leagues again. And a lot of it was because of him and Bill Monbouquette.

BRENT GAFF: Bambie liked me, and I liked anybody that liked me back. I don't know, he was awful old to be a manager [Bamberger was 59 years old in 1982]. The favorite guy that I had was Bill Monbouquette - he kind of took me under his wing, and taught me the mental aspect of the game. I remember in A Ball, the first dinger in A Ball, I shook the guy's hand at home plate. And my manager said, "What did you tell him?" "I told him, *'Nice shot'*." And he pinned me to the wall by my throat, he said, "What the fuck's wrong with you, kid?" But if I hit anybody in high school or anywhere else, I always apologized - I didn't mean to. Or if they hit a home run, I'd say, "Hey, nice shot buddy. I'll just strike you out the next three times." But that was not the right mentality for professional ball, and I learned the hard way.

RICK OWNBEY: I was very comfortable with him, because of my particular journey of really the only time I played real organized baseball was in the junior college, and then I get drafted in June and played half a season of A Ball, and then I play one full season at Double A, and then I only played up until August of Triple A. In a two-year period after I got drafted, I was pitching in the big leagues for the Mets. And George was a very good manager - he tried to make me feel comfortable, which would be a big advantage in my particular situation.

STEVE JACOBSON: I thought that Bamberger was not right for the job. Cashen brought him from Baltimore, where he had been a very good pitching coach, and it didn't make the Mets better.

PETE FALCONE: Nothing [in response to being asked "What did George Bamberger bring to the team?"]. To you, what stands out? Nothing against George personally, he was a good guy. It was just a time where, "We've got to blame someone. Let's blame the manager and get a new manager." Which they do a lot in sports. But George didn't do anything.

PAT ZACHRY: Hard working man. I wasn't sure after his heart problems that he wanted to take us on. But apparently, it wasn't that big a deal for him!

MIKE TORREZ: One of the reasons I went to the Mets was because of George Bamberger, who was a great gentleman. I knew that he enjoyed the game and had fun, and always kidded with you. He was always that kind of a manager - you could communicate with him and get along with him. The same with Hondo - Frank Howard. He was easygoing and I liked him as a person, and as a manager, he was, "Let's go guys, let's win this game!" He was always "Mr. Positive." He was a good guy also to play for. I enjoyed my year with those two managers - both first class people, who had pride in winning.

CHAPTER 15:
MAZZILLI

GARY "BABA BOOEY" DELL'ABATE: That was a big deal in our house, because we were Italian and he was from the part of Brooklyn where we came from. And he was a young, good-looking guy. I remember I go back and look at some of those things now - the uniform was *way too tight* on that guy! That was at the time that the Mets started wearing those double knit uniforms. But he was awesome. He was a really good player.

BOBBY VALENTINE: Lee Mazzilli was "the chosen one." He was from Brooklyn, he had the flair, he had the looks, he was a switch-hitter, he could run, catch balls, steal bases. He was everything every fan could ever want - especially every New York fan. He did all of what he did with style and grace, and without a lot of help on the team. He was really special.

STEVE JACOBSON: A lot of flash and not a lot of substance. He came as a local hero, he was the "Italian Stallion," and he was good looking and an attractive figure for the girls of New York. But he was an overrated prospect. He wasn't going to come in and be "Mickey Mantle" again. He was going to be Mazzilli, and he was around for a couple of years, and he was gone. I was ultimately very surprised when he became a coach in the Yankee system [under Torre, from 2000-2003, and again in 2006].

LENNY RANDLE: Mays says, "You teach Maz how to bunt!" I go, "OK. So, second, third, and short, that's my area. I'll work with Maz on it." And I go, "Maz, you're going to have to get two cars - park one in the bullpen and one in the alley. Because you're like the Beatles! You've got groupies everywhere! What do you wear? What kind of cologne are you wearing?" And Joe Pignatano goes, "As long as you don't step on my tomatoes [Pignatano had a garden in the bullpen], you can park that car anywhere you want!"

CRAIG SWAN: No doubt, he was definitely kind of a "Rocky." He had long hair and was a good-looking guy, and had that New York accent. A little bit shy, but he was attractive I'm sure - especially for the young girls. He didn't do much for me, but that's the way it goes. [Laughs]

PETE FALCONE: In the early '70s, I went to Lafayette High School, in Brooklyn. And Lee went to Lincoln High School, which was in Coney Island - near Sheepshead Bay. So Lafayette and Lincoln, they were in our conference, so we had *battles,* y'know? Then Lee and I would play together on our sandlot team, and we had a great team. Oh man, we had an All-Star team. And people don't realize that Lee Mazzilli could have been in the Olympics as a skater. You went in Lee's room - many years ago - and he had medals and trophies for skating. Not even baseball. I was a senior and he was a junior. I got drafted and I went and played baseball after junior college, but when he got signed in '73, he was the first round pick [by the Mets].

When he came up to the big leagues, I was in St. Louis. He came up late in the '76 season, and they nurtured him - they took care of him. Which they had to. But in '79, when I went to the Mets, he was "the hometown boy," and rightly so. He played centerfield, he batted third or led off at times, a switch-hitter. Lee had one of the best eyes at home plate that I recall of anybody. He knew the strike zone like anybody did, and hit the ball good on both sides of the plate. He was colorful out there. He wasn't really a "hot dog" - he was just a kind of guy that brought people to the stadium. People don't realize that even though we didn't draw great, people came to see Lee Mazzilli and came to see the Mets because of Lee Mazzilli a lot of times. All the success he got, he earned it and he deserved it. And he was one of the bright spots in the organization.

JOHN STEARNS: He was an Italian kid from New York, so there was a big hype there. And Lee was a talented hitter - a switch-hitter who could run. I thought he was a talented player. It turned out he wasn't as talented as maybe everybody had hoped when he came up, but we went with Lee for three or four years as the everyday centerfielder.

PAT ZACHRY: Wonderful fella. Just wished he'd had an arm. Lee could go get it in centerfield as good as anybody. I'm not going to sit here and tell you he was a bad outfielder, but he just didn't have much of an arm. That's never going to sound right, that's never going to come out right, I don't even know how else to say it - he just didn't have much of an arm. Could go get 'em as good as anybody I ever saw. He could run and catch it as good as anybody I ever saw.

But he threw across his body, and they tried to get people to work with him - they tried to get Willie to work with him all the time - and he didn't have much success throwing. But as far as going and getting it, he was one of the best I ever saw. He could go and get it without being second to anybody. But he just couldn't throw. Was a good hitter - switch hit. If he'd have had any other position than centerfield, he could have really made himself a great ballplayer. And a hell of a guy. Loved his dad - his mother and father were really super people. And Lee was a hell of a nice guy.

JEFF REARDON: Mazzilli was pretty impressive those years. I thought he'd have a much better career, but I think

New York built him up too much. He was supposed to be like, "the next Mickey Mantle." I mean, there ain't too many Mickey Mantles around. I think that made it hard on Maz. He was a good, average player - he had a little power, he could run, but they built him up way too much.

LENNY RANDLE: Lee Mazzilli was a very shy player, who was kind of a "Sonny Bono kind of guy" coming into the limelight, or a "Donny Osmond kind of guy," and was adjusting. He was a teenager in a major league body. He hadn't even played a hundred games in high school or pro at all. So Willie says, "Hang with him and bring him along. Let him hang with you guys." I think we were the youngest guys on the team - with Roy Lee Jackson, Steve Henderson, Doug Flynn, Joel Youngblood. We could relate to his maturing at the plate.

And we just said, "They don't know you. You just swing at the first thing you see that's a fastball - don't take! You see a fastball, just stroke it, because you're a switch-hitter. And we're going to have an advantage if we bat back-to-back around each other, because they don't know how to pitch you yet. So, worse case scenario, you bunt, because you can fly. We can bunt, hit-and-run, get you to third, or you can go deep, because you have that kind of ability. But don't try to do it all in one game. If you go 0-3 or 0-4, don't worry about it - just think good contact and don't strikeout. Put everything in play, because you've got better odds when you put it in play. I have not seen a guy get to the big leagues walking yet - it's not happening. So hack, swing at whatever you see. Be like Yogi - if you can see it, *hit it.*"

So, it took his aggressiveness to that level and it made him more successful with hitting. Even though he had a great eye for walks, once he got on, with his speed, he could steal bases, as well. And he could get some "leg hits" in, in the infield. He didn't have to come in and be a Mickey Mantle, or a big power hitter like Carlos Beltrán or somebody like that. He could stay within himself and mature gradually. Then after he got a hundred games in, he just blossomed into an All-Star.

CRAIG SWAN: I think Maz was [the Mets' top player during the late '70s/early '80s], absolutely.

GARY "BABA BOOEY" DELL'ABATE: A postscript to that is Mazzilli is one of my neighbors. I see him periodically around town. He'll recognize me and we'll chat for a second or two, and I'm so thrilled by that, because I was such a huge fan.

CHAPTER 16:
KINGMAN

GARY "BABA BOOEY" DELL'ABATE: I remember that he came to the Mets, and again, this is all pre-Internet, so you it's not like Dave Kingman came to the Mets and you looked up [his stats]. Dave Kingman came to the Mets and you looked in the paper, and you read either the Daily News or the New York Post - I certainly wasn't reading the New York Times as a kid - and then my dad would fill in the blanks. I remember, my dad said to me, "He's either going to hit home runs or strikeout. That's pretty much it. And he's a pretty crappy fielder." And that was pretty right on - my dad seemed to be right on for that one.

The problem with Dave Kingman was, hitting four home runs in a 16-0 win or a 16-10 loss - he never seemed to be a difference maker. He hit a lot of home runs when you didn't need them one way or the other - you didn't need them because you were losing so bad or you were so winning so big. But I do remember his home runs were *massive.* I remember his home runs better once he got traded to the Cubs [for whom Kingman played for from 1978-1980], and then they would all land in the street.

STEVE JACOBSON: He was not a good baseball player. He could hit monumental home runs - he hit a home run off of Gossage in spring training that Gossage just marveled at. But Kingman couldn't play a position, and he couldn't really do anything else but hit home runs and be uncomfortable doing other things.

JOHN STEARNS: Dave Kingman was a unique player, in that he had more raw power than anybody I've ever seen.

By "raw power," I mean he could hit a ball further than anybody I know - even now, with today's players. And yet, he struck out a lot, he didn't hit for average, and he just had kind of an aloof personality and demeanor. He was aloof to the point where you didn't know if he even cared about playing, which, I think he did, but didn't show much emotion one way or another. He probably led the league in strikeouts all those years that he was there.

But yet, he had that unique ability that nobody else had. He just had tremendous raw power, so if you're looking for that in a player, he's extremely exciting. The fans loved him. He'd hit 35 home runs, but he'd strikeout 150 times. The other thing about him is he was extremely talented in all areas, and he didn't use it. He could run, he could throw, and play defense. This guy could do some things, and yet, he didn't show it to you. He didn't show anybody that. I don't want to be critical of Dave Kingman - he was a great power hitter. But the total game should have been better I thought, than what it was.

TIM McCARVER: The word out was that Kong was a problem - problem this, problem that. *I found him delightful.* As a matter of fact, we became very friendly. As a broadcaster…it's not dangerous or anything like that, but it's not a broadcaster's job to be a friend of the players. I was friendly with quite a few, and Dave Kingman was one of them. I was also not on good terms with a few - like Jeff Kent [who played for the Mets from 1992-1996]. Jeff and I never got along. They would listen to the games on the air and all that, and hear it from their friends - "McCarver's doing this" and "McCarver's doing that." So I, as a broadcaster, was similar to Dave Kingman. So we were kindred spirits, in a sense, and we became very friendly and we would go out to dinner on the road. I rarely did that with players. But I have a soft spot in my heart for Dave Kingman.

BRENT GAFF: When I first came up, I wound up walking to the park with him a couple of times. And he was one of the guys that really kind of treated me nice and was like, "Look rookie, *here's what's happening.* Here's how you get to the ballpark, for one. And here's what we're doing." Yeah, Kingman was good about that. But some of the older guys, they didn't want...y'know, Seaver hated rookies - although I fished with Tom Seaver. He kind of liked me because I liked to fish. We fished in spring training a few times together. But normally, him and Rusty Staub - Staub hated me, I know. He hated rookies too, but I don't blame him. After being there for ten years like those guys were, you're like, "Here come these dumb kids that don't know how to act."

TOM GORMAN: I was only up there for about a month [in 1982], so I never really got to see Dave "do his thing." I know it was kind of a fiasco for him in '83 - he had a lot of strikeouts and the fans weren't exactly favorable to him. Dave and I were good friends. Actually, when my wife went back to Oregon, I stayed with him at the lake - Lake Hopatcong [in New Jersey]. So Dave and I became very good friends. I still to this day talk to him - he lives in Tahoe, so I talk to him occasionally. He has some relatives up in Seattle, so he swings in here.

WALT TERRELL: Great teammate. I heard different things, that he wasn't, and at the time I was with them, I was like, "I don't know who said this" - never got any of that. He was willing to throw early BP to guys, would be out doing things early. I just thoroughly loved being around him. I always thought, "God, why wouldn't the Red Sox sign this guy? Shit, he might hit *75 home runs a year* if he played in Fenway!" Great teammate. Hit some long home runs, and was very good to me. I hated to see him go, but I know how things are. Good teammate, will always think that way - very nice man.

BOBBY VALENTINE: Dave Kingman, just a great guy. Misunderstood. He liked living on his boat and being alone as much as he liked standing ovations after hitting towering home runs. A really fine person, who cared about his teammates, and had some of the most incredible power of anybody I had ever seen. He was an "inconsistent right-handed Darryl Strawberry."

MIKE TORREZ: He had his boat right on the marina, right by the stadium, where he stayed, I believe - he lived on the boat, and would walk right over to the stadium. Dave was quiet - he never bothered anybody. He'd laugh once in a while. He was not a prankster or anything. He took the game serious and was a great teammate. I liked him.

JERRY KOOSMAN: A very strong man. Gosh, he could hit a ball a long ways, and even do it one-handed - I saw him hit a few one-handed! [Laughs] And he had some natural ability there. He was a fast runner, he could lay down a bunt and beat it out, and there were some times when he got into some hitting slumps and struck out a lot - I tried to talk him into just bunting once or twice, to help him get through the slump. When he was hot, he was really something to watch. But when he was cold, it was tough.

PETE FALCONE: For most of Kingman's career, it was feast or famine. He wasn't going to hit a groundball base hit to the opposite field. He wasn't going to hit a line drive over the first baseman's head and go for two. It was either feast or famine with Kingman. And that's what he was paid to do - to hit home runs. You'd see him in batting practice, it was scary. He'd put that fear in a pitcher - a pitcher does *not* want to give up a home run that goes 550 feet. And I've seen him do it. It was something to watch.

I just wish he would have had other guys around him, to really help him. He kind of had that in Chicago, but in New York, I think he had George behind him, which really helped him, but if George wasn't there, who was going to protect Kingman? They'd pitch around Kingman, and maybe face a Hubie Brooks. There was nobody there. I wish Dave would have hit 500 [Kingman hit a total of 442 homers in his career]. If he'd have hit 500 home runs, he'd be in the Hall of Fame - even with a .230 batting average.

STEVE JACOBSON: You didn't want to talk to him [as a reporter]. He was a University of Southern California player - he played on good baseball teams in college, he was also a pitcher. He was not somebody you wanted to go to - he was cranky, much more than he should have been. You'd take a pass on cranky players who were very good, and he wasn't. People used to play tricks on him. He was very tall, and when they were going on the road, somebody had hid his underwear - his undershorts - and I remember him walking around like a giraffe, looking on top of the other lockers for his underwear.

JEFF REARDON: I remember Wally Backman flipping him on his ass in the clubhouse! [Laughs] Wally was a state championship wrestler at Oregon, and I think Kingman was kidding him - here's Kingman at what, 6' 6", and Wally is what, 5' 8"? And Wally was like, "Yeah, I was pretty good." "Oh, let's go at it out here." And Wally, I think he pinned him in like 30 seconds or something. We thought that was funny. Kingman wasn't a nice guy - not to me…not just to me, but younger guys. He did not like pitchers at all, but I didn't care, because that drove me when I pitched against him after he left. But I'd never seen a guy hit a ball so far in my life - until I met him. That's the one thing that stands out. Yeah, he struck out, but boy, he had some power.

SKIP LOCKWOOD: David carried our team for weeks on his back - singly, as a hitter. I remember him going to the plate two or three times - not only would they have to play him deep, but they'd have to play him to leftfield. And I think that helped the team a lot, because we would be able to run in front of him and score runs - even if he got a single, the guy would score from first, because they had to play him differently in the outfield. David was a really good hitter. I remember him as an uppercut hitter, a big swing hitter. A big, rangy guy. David was a friend of mine. We came to the ballpark some days together. He was a good guy.

PAT ZACHRY: He was a wonderful teammate. I wished he could have hit for average a little bit better, but he hit what, .230 or something he hit he home run title? [Kingman actually hit .208 in 1982] He could be pitched to, but my gosh, if you made a mistake, geez, the guy hit such prodigious home runs. A good teammate though, a good guy to have around. Just really easygoing, as far as I was concerned.

CHAPTER 17: FOSTER

CRAIG SWAN: Unfortunately, when George got over here, he didn't have the kind of line-up surrounding him that he did in the Reds. So they pitched around him pretty much. George was swinging at balls in the dirt, because they weren't giving him anything to hit. When you've got Johnny Bench and Dan Driessen, they've got to pitch to you, because the other guys are so good. So unfortunately for George, he got pitched around. I think he put a lot of pressure on himself with the amount of money they paid him, and it just didn't work out for him.

PETE FALCONE: George is a great guy. I was happy to have him there. I was looking forward to seeing him in spring training, I remember. Because pitching to him in the mid '70s was like, *"This is something here."* You had very little room for error with George. But by the time he got to New York, he didn't have that bat speed. He was missing something. And there was nobody hitting around him. At least in Cincinnati, he had Johnny Bench, Tony Pérez, and Joe Morgan. So you had to pitch to those guys. But he wasn't the same guy. But he was in great shape, and he would hit balls 450 feet, eight feet off the ground. But it really didn't do much for the team. It was good to have him in the line-up. And the few times it did click, there were times when him and Kingman were batting fourth and fifth, which was really something. But the consistency wasn't there no more, definitely.

JOHN STEARNS: It was astounding, because I think the Mets finally came around and gave him probably the richest contract up to that point in time that anybody had ever gotten. He got a five-year contract for $10 million. And nobody had ever had a contract like that. So we got George, and he'd hit 50 home runs for Cincinnati a couple of years earlier. I had been playing against him, and he just showed up and played leftfield for us, and I think that first year, he hit like, ten home runs [Foster hit a total of 13 homers in '82]. It was like it was a huge surprise that he didn't show up and give us the power and the player that we thought he was.

But what can you say? He was out there trying all the time. It just shows you, first of all, Shea Stadium is a very hard ballpark to hit in. It was a very deep park. It was just not a good hitter's park at all. And Foster came over there and couldn't hit home runs. I don't know what happened, but he never really put together even close to the kind of year that he had a couple of years in a row with Cincinnati. It just goes to show you, you're young and you come up, and you've got guys like Rose and Morgan and Pérez hitting around you, it shows you what can happen to a young player. And Foster became one of the best power hitters in the game then. And then when he got traded over to the Mets, and he was having to hit in the four spot every day and he was "the guy," it just wasn't there. We were all shocked watching it happen, that he would come over and just hit ten home runs. I'm sure the Mets were shocked too, because at that time, he got a really huge contract.

CHARLIE PULEO: I think it could be a number of different things. Sometimes, your skills, you get a little older and you can't catch up like you used to. But a lot of pressure playing in New York. Cincinnati's a great market, the time the Big Red Machine was playing, it was *packed* - they were playing in front of big crowds. But New York is a different story. George, if he jaywalked in the street, it was on the back page of the Daily News. It's a little different. I think there was a combination of that. It wasn't the "George

Foster years of his prime," but they were still good years, and he was very productive in New York.

RANDY JONES: I was pretty excited to have George in the line-up. A real professional. He went about his business in the right way and still had unbelievable power. But it really seemed like...I don't know if the line-up didn't protect him or he was getting the pitches that were necessary, but he never came back to that brilliance that you saw when he was with the Reds. But still, he showed up every single day and you'd have never known it, from the way he approached the game and the way he played it, and working with all the young players.

CHARLIE PULEO: I talked more pitching on the bench with George than I talked with anybody. He'd sit me down, and I was a young guy, and we'd talk about hitters and how to pitch them, and guys that he'd been around. He was a great guy in the clubhouse. New York's a tough place to play - I wish he had gotten off to a better start, because he was a heck of a player. He deserved more appreciation than he did get while he was there.

GARY "BABA BOOEY" DELL'ABATE: I think he was probably doomed to fail from the minute he got there. I thought it was a big signing, but probably not the right signing, because he was a very, very good player, but not the great, great player. I remember those ridiculous muttonchop sideburns of his! If he didn't come in and play like, with ridiculous numbers, he was never going to satisfy the fans. And that's sort of what happened. A lot of people pinned everything that went wrong on him, but I thought it was unfair. It's not his fault that they offered him a lot of money and he took it. It's *their* stupidity.

CRAIG SWAN: They gave it a good try with George - George just didn't work out. But then they got Keith, and then they got Gary, and that seemed to do it.

CHAPTER 18: STEARNS

RANDY JONES: John was beautiful - we called him "The Bad Dude." *Bad Dude Stearns.* He showed up and had a lot of fire, a lot of energy back there. Just a good teammate. Ready to play, and played the game right. He could be pretty serious during the game, but a pretty loose guy after that. I enjoyed having John as a teammate. I had a picture that I got from an AP photographer from San Diego that I got John to autograph for me. It was me sliding into second base - I'd missed a signal when I was on first, and I stole a base off of John Stearns! And I had a big picture of me sliding into second base against the Mets. I remember bringing that picture into the clubhouse one day, and said, "Hey John, you were catching this day. Do you mind autographing this for me?" He laughed and was screaming at me as he was signing it - but I still got it!

JOHN STEARNS: Around 1970, I went out to lunch with a writer from Sports Illustrated, who was in town to research our team, at the University of Colorado - our football team. He came down during the spring of my freshman season. Freshmen were not eligible back then. But as a freshman, you become eligible for the varsity in spring football. So in spring football, I was the only freshman in the class that was on the starting team. A writer came in from Sports Illustrated to research our team, because we were going to be in next fall's top-20 preseason list. I don't know why, but the sports information director had me go out to lunch with this guy - along with another senior player.

So I'm out to lunch with this writer, and he says, "John, what do you want to be remembered as?" And I say, "Well, I want to hit people out there - that's what football is. I want to be remembered as *a bad dude.*" It was just an off-the-cuff thing that I said to his writer. So the next fall, we were ranked maybe twelfth or tenth in that issue, and they had a one-page write-up on each of those teams. And I hadn't even played in a game yet, and I'm the main guy in this article! Yeah, I did start at free safety at Colorado my sophomore year, but it was after this thing came out - in Sports Illustrated, in that article, he called me "Bad Dude Stearns." Now, that happened in 1970. I cannot get rid of that - it's still with me today! It was with me in New York with the Mets, I can't lose it. So there it is - it's forty-something years later, and you're bringing up "bad dude."

STEVE JACOBSON: Very tough. He was a football player, and he brought some of that attitude to the Mets. He was…the cliché is "firebrand," I'm not sure what a firebrand is, but he was a pusher and full of "Go get 'em." He was a very good player in that way.

SKIP LOCKWOOD: John Stearns was coming in, he was a big strong kid - a football player. He caught a different way than Grote did. I mean, Grote was a two-handed catcher, and I liked the way Jerry framed the plate for me. Jerry and I had good communication. Stearns was coming in and he was just coming to be an All-Star player when I was there. I must have thrown to him quite a bit, but I do remember the times when I threw to Jerry Grote being the best that I could pitch. I remember Stearns was there and I probably threw to him more than I realize, but I remember the days with Grote more.

PAT ZACHRY: Please don't take this the wrong way - you had to have *somebody* on the All-Star team. During those years, [Stearns] was the only one playing worth a darn. We also had Ron Hodges - it was his back up. You couldn't find a better catcher. He didn't hit as well as Stearns did, but Ronnie knew everybody, and he was very easy to pitch to.

JOHN STEARNS: Making the All-Star team was a great honor [Stearns would make the All-Star team four times as a Met - 1977, 1979, 1980, and 1982]. I never thought I would play in a Major League All-Star Game, growing up in Denver - even though I was a little league player that felt I could play in the big leagues. But being in the All-Star Game was a great thrill and a great honor. I was grateful for that. Even though I never started in an All-Star Game, I certainly was appreciative of the fact that I was playing there and it was a great thrill. I played in...'77 was Yankee Stadium, '79 was Seattle, '80 was Los Angeles, and '82 was Montreal. It was a big thrill going to the game and that really solidified my feeling that I was a "big league guy."

STEVE HENDERSON: As far as Stearns, Stearns was outstanding. He helped me get my first apartment, as a matter of fact! I was grateful for John Stearns.

JEFF REARDON: He wanted to be in control of the whole game. I remember shaking him off once, and he came out to the mound, and he sort of gave me the finger on my chest, like, *"Don't be shaking me off, rookie."* And I just swatted his hand away, and said, "Get back and catch!" I ended up throwing the pitch I wanted to, anyways. He never did it again, I'll tell you that. [Laughs] But I would call him "a gamer." Him and Mazzilli.

BRENT GAFF: I couldn't throw to him. He knew way more than I did. He caught me in Triple A too, sometimes. Him and Rick Sweet. I knew how I wanted to pitch, and I always had good success with people that were on the same page with me. But when I threw to Stearns or Sweet, it was nothing but a big argument - the whole game. I would shake off, and they would shake their head "Yes," and I would shake off. And a lot of times, I got hit. I never really got along good with Stearns. I mean, I liked John as a person, but I couldn't throw to him.

I couldn't throw to Gary, God bless his soul. I wasn't a power pitcher - I had to have corners given. I could hit the glove every time. Gary set that pecker high, right down the middle, every time, no matter what was coming. And I said, "Gary, that's *the last place* I want to throw it." It was blowing my mind - I had never pitched like this before. He said, "Just aim at my kneecaps. Aim at my shin guards." I don't know, when you're doing something for like, seven or eight years, and this is how I do it...Ron Hodges caught me earlier, they let Hodges handle me. And Hodges would give me a target, and I threw good to him. But every time I threw to Stearns or Carter, I got lit up.

CHARLIE PULEO: I enjoyed throwing to John. And I enjoyed Ron Hodges. He was a great defensive catcher. John was known more for his hitting - he was a .300 hitter. He was very knowledgeable and I don't think in all the time he caught me down there, I never thought about shaking him off. He was a leader in the clubhouse and a leader in the field, and a heck of a player. But very good to throw to, and Ron Hodges was the same - both good catchers.

BOBBY VALENTINE: John liked to take charge. He wanted to be the captain type guy on the team. Always had a football mentality when he played. Was frustrated that he didn't hit with power, but he could compete with anybody who ever had a bat in their hand. He would battle the pitcher and block the ball in the dirt, and put his face in front of it if he had to. And one time, even put his face in front of Dave Parker's helmet, and held onto the ball when all that was said and done. John Stearns was a very good guy who competed with everyone around him at all times.

JOHN STEARNS: It was a fun season [when Stearns served as the Mets' bench coach in 2000, when Valentine was the manager]. We felt that we could compete all along. We had Mike Piazza - I was coaching Mike. Mike, of course, was an offensive type of player. I couldn't push him that much defensively - he was playing a lot at that position, and still hitting. What we tried to do with Mike is to try to keep the ball in front, and try to work on his defense as much as we could, but because he played so much, it was hard to get him out there to even practice that much, because he was catching every night and playing about 160 games. There's no DH in the National League, so you had to have his bat in there. So he had to catch a lot. That was taxing on him physically.

See, the thing about catching is this - you've got to make nine throw-downs per game, between innings. When your pitcher ends his warm-up pitches, you have to throw the ball down. Nine times a game, you have to throw from home to second. And they stopped taking infield practice by the time he played, but your arm is taxed as a catcher. And people don't realize that - how hard it is to go out there and make nine throws to second base every day, before you even throw in the game. And then, of course, you've got 120 throws back to the pitcher every day. Your arm never feels really good as a catcher. And for a guy like Johnny Bench to have had as good an arm as he did - and Iván Rodríguez - to be able to throw like that and catch every day, it's just incredible. I had a plus-type of arm, but it was nowhere near those guys. And my arm was really taxed from all the throwing that we had to do.

The World Series with the Yankees, it was disappointing for us - I thought we could take it to seven games and maybe win it. But we didn't get over the hump with them. Joe Torre was the manager for the Yankees - that was strange, because he was my manager with the Mets. And they had a real good team. Wasn't that the Series where Piazza went out towards the mound with Clemens? We didn't like Clemens. He thought he was a badass. He's a great, big, huge guy. He threw 98 miles an hour every time, and he was extremely agitated on the mound when he pitched. I can see that - that's the way I like to play. But he was *extremely* agitated.

I had heard that phrase ["The monster is out of the cage!"] from someone else. I don't know who it was. So Piazza...I forget what happened, didn't he win a game? [Piazza hit a run-scoring double in Game 1 of the 2000 NLCS, against the St. Louis Cardinals] "The monster is out of the cage," I think it was a funny quote that I had just heard recently from somebody, so it fit the situation right there. I said it, and people heard it. I didn't think it was even that big of a deal. I think it said a lot about Mike and how we all were in awe of his abilities to hit the baseball and hit for power, and play his position.

STEVE HENDERSON: I thought he was a great player. I thought he was outstanding. He was an All-Star and one of the best catchers I have been around, that I know. I had a lot of respect for John.

CHAPTER 19:
SWAN & ZACHRY

STEVE HENDERSON: I thought Swanie was one of those pitchers that a lot of people overlook. He had good stuff, he swung the bat real well, and I thought he was an outstanding pitcher. You ask for somebody to battle and win a ballgame - that was Craig Swan.

DAN NORMAN: He was a hard worker. I thought he threw well, good pitch selection. He managed the game pretty good when he was out there on the mound.

STEVE JACOBSON: He was a pretty good, gutty pitcher. He was not a #1 pitcher, but he would be a regular starter and a very useful pitcher. And he was a student of Seaver.

LENNY RANDLE: Craig was phenomenal at Arizona State. We had a great time watching him imitate Tom Seaver, basically, in college. And then he goes to the Mets, and he's going, "Lenny, hey, we got this. Just come over here and have fun - you're going to love the city. Just pick everything you can - third, second, whatever. Do 'ASU defense' and we'll be fine!" It was like, "Then just don't thrown any strikes," because our thing in Arizona State was, "Don't throw strikes. Throw nip - inside two inches or three inches outside." Because that's how we went to the College World Series [in 1972] - we had great pitching. So that tutelage from him and [ASU baseball coach] Bobby Winkles transferred into the Mets' system, with Rube Walker, who was the pitching coach. That good tutelage from college helped him keep his mind on how to pitch like a Picasso. He was "painting" that year [1978]. He was a painter. He was van Gogh. He was LeRoy Neiman.

BOBBY VALENTINE: I remember when he pitched, we were always pulling for those runs to stay off of the board towards the end of the season, because Swanie was just one of those great guys, who was always chuckling and being nice to everyone. Except for when he pitched - he was a bulldog when he pitched.

JERRY KOOSMAN: Swanie threw well. He had a good fastball, he was a strong pitcher. He was one of our regular starters - that's for sure.

CHARLIE PULEO: Craig was another one of those "veteran guys," like Randy Jones, Pat Zachry, Pete Falcone - all veteran guys. I remember Craig pitched a lot of really good ballgames, where he didn't get a whole lot of support, as far as offensively.

WALT TERRELL: Swanie was kind of...I hate to say "on the downside," because I was on the downside my whole damn career, so I hate to use that phrase! But a little older, losing some stuff, so to speak, but willing to talk and willing to help. All those kinds of things. A sad day when Craig Swan got released, as far as I was concerned. I know he had been with the Mets a long time, and was very fortunate to be around him, and go out and have a beer with him once in a while - those kinds of things. A guy I will always remember being a positive, good person, and glad I got to be a teammate of his.

RANDY JONES: Swanie was a beauty. He was really throwing the baseball well, and you've got to remember, I go all the way back to the early '70s in Anchorage, Alaska - we were teammates. We were on the same semi-pro team up in Anchorage. So I've known Craig a long, long time. To rejoin him there, he was just a great guy. Loved to pitch and I loved his work ethic. He always worked them down in the strike zone, and in the bullpen he worked really hard on it. I just remember every fifth day when he'd pitch, he had that game face on when he walked in. I'll never forget it. He was like a different animal that day - I really enjoyed that with Craig.

RICK OWNBEY: At that point, I definitely looked up to them [Swan and Zachry] as the leaders on the team. The veteran players. There was no doubt that they were pulling for you - they were not trying to make your life tougher or hold things back. Good players and good people. They liked the challenge - I was no threat to them. If I went forward, they were going to be happy for me. But tremendous help along the way for me.

RANDY JONES: Zachry was one of those guys that was a little bit laid back. A Texas boy. And pitched with a lot of intensity, but he never really got back to that form that we saw when he was with the Reds. He'd make mistakes, he might elevate a baseball. He just never got back in that good groove. There were some injuries that plagued him, and he just never quite put it together at Shea Stadium.

BOBBY VALENTINE: He was a great guy, with a great changeup. He was a Rookie of the Year, that really had high promise. He was one of the first starting pitchers - I think along with Andy Messersmith and Al Downing - that believed enough in his changeup to make it one of his major pitches.

DAN NORMAN: It seems to me like he took the ball every fifth day, when I was there. Good guy, threw well. Luck plays a lot of the part in baseball, too. Sometimes they say it's a game of inches - yeah, it is. It could have been an out, which winds up being a hit - just a couple of inches away. I thought he pitched good.

CHARLIE PULEO: Pat was another guy that took me [under his wing]. I remember one time, he and his wife took me and my wife out in New York somewhere down in Greenwich Village - I had just been in the big leagues for a couple of weeks in New York. And he showed us around. He was real nice to us. That was Pat. I think in New York, he had some injuries that hurt him. He had good stuff. When he was "on," he had that heavy sinker which was unhittable. I think injuries bothered him more in New York than a lot of people knew about. But an outstanding guy, and an outstanding teammate, also.

PAT ZACHRY: Well, it's hard for me to say [if Zachry feels that the Mets got good players in return for Seaver]. He went over there to Cincinnati and did real well. He would have done well had he stayed in New York. He would have made the most of it - he was going to be a Hall of Fame pitcher. Whether or not he would have gotten along with M. Donald was another idea. Hindsight is always 20/20 - I didn't think M. Donald was that good a fella, myself. It's a tough call to make. History gives you all kinds of ammunition, as far as Seaver's case goes. And as far as the other man goes, well, maybe it's a good thing for him that he got rid of Seaver. So, I think everybody won out in the end.

CRAIG SWAN: Oh yeah [in response to being asked, "Do you ever wonder how your career would have been different if you didn't suffer so many injuries?"]. I had *so many* arm injuries. And the way they protect their pitchers now - they don't let them throw over a hundred pitches anymore. That was nothing for us. We used to go nine innings and throw 160. I pitched a game when I was in the minor leagues, I pitched 14 innings - I have no idea how many pitches I threw. I don't think they'd let a starter go 14 down in the minors anymore! It was just different back then. The starters were usually your best pitchers, and you didn't have all these specialty guys to come in and mop up the seventh and the eighth, and a new guy comes in for the ninth. It's different now.

PAT ZACHRY: As far as it goes, my baseball life didn't turn out as well as I wanted it to, but everything else sure as hell has. I've been a pretty lucky guy - I doubt if there's many of them that can say they've been as fortunate as I have. I'm married to the same woman all these years - she's put up with me all these years. We have a couple of kids and four grandchildren. It's just been a wonderful life. None of it would have happened had I done anything else any differently. I was lucky enough to flunk the physical for the draft in 1971 - there I was, I was 19 years old, I was in A Ball, and I couldn't even pass the physical for the Armed Forces. So, thank goodness that happens, and I eventually make it to the major leagues, and stay there for ten years. I got to coach a couple of years with some guys out of the minor league teams that I was with, from the Dodgers - there was probably six or seven, maybe eight guys off of those teams that made it to the major leagues. Everything has been a plus.

CHAPTER 20:
STRAWBERRY &
GOODEN

MIKE FITZGERALD: I liked Darryl a lot. We're both Southern California guys, and I always felt like Darryl had a really good heart. Not only did he have a really good heart, but he had a lot of talent. He could do things that other guys could only dream about - mainly hitting the ball. But he played good defense and he did everything extremely well. He carried the burden of the spotlight more than most very good major league players do. Darryl was under the microscope all the time, and I think that that may have been a little weight on his shoulders - whether it was warranted or not, it just happens, where it happens to certain players.

As far as Dwight goes, I can never remember one negative thing about that guy. I can't remember one bad thing about Dwight Gooden. He was always on time, always ready for his game, always was focused for his day to pitch. Not only was he fantastic to catch, but he was a good person and I just really liked Dwight a lot. I enjoyed catching him, and I felt like if we ever didn't win the game that he started, that the other team was extremely lucky to somehow get away with it.

STEVE ZABRISKIE: I think Darryl brought a lot. But it was a little early for Darryl, and that might have been the one thing, if I can be critical - I have a hard time being critical, because so much of what happened was so good and worked - I think they did rush Darryl just a little bit. I don't know if he was emotionally mature or professionally mature as a player. But he had such immense talent. And he was such a draw. And he was "the straw the stirred the drink" in many ways. I would have loved to see them wait until '84 to bring him up, because coming up in the middle of the year - whether it's early or late in the year - it's not easy. And of course, in New York with the media and the expectations that he had...I admire him for the way he did handle it. But it was very, very difficult for him. And that would be expected. But the guy made a difference, there's no question about that. He has *immense* talent.

I've seen him off and on in years since - we have really good conversations. I appreciate what he's been through and where he is now a great deal, because he's in a much better place. It's really a shame what happened to him [Strawberry and Gooden both suffered from drug addiction at various points, and found themselves in trouble with the law and/or incarcerated], because it was such a waste from a standpoint of what his career could have been like. And that's the sadness of when that happens, because it's so pervasive. But I really think that he also elevated the ballclub, because he was such a huge talent. But it was not easy for him to be a leader. He didn't know yet how to do that. He knew that he had a lot of responsibility on his shoulders, and the pressure was there for him to perform. And even though some guys had looked to him because of his talent and his role to be a leader, it was really hard for him, because he didn't know how to do that. He eventually figured it out, but I think it would have been better for him to come up at the beginning of '84.

GARY "BABA BOOEY" DELL'ABATE: I remember hearing that the Mets had signed him even before he took the field, and it being a big deal that the Mets had gotten this really special player. It's not like football, where you get the #1 pick out of college and everybody knows who it is. I just remember everybody talking about how "This guy is a really special player." He was the guy that would hit some booming home runs, and when you're watching baseball, that's like a touchdown. There's home runs, and then there's ones that just keep *going.* And when he would hit the ones that would keep going, you knew he was special.

RICK OWNBEY: Keep in mind, the #1 pick in 1980 was Darryl Strawberry. If I'm not wrong, he went to Macon, Georgia, for an A Ball team [Strawberry actually played in Lynchburg, Virginia for A Ball], and I didn't see it, but I was told that they had rented a helicopter and dropped strawberries on the field. I always thought, "Talk about some pressure!" I mean, that's a unique situation right there.

PETE FALCONE: I remember going to Los Angeles with the team, we were playing the Dodgers, and Darryl came into the clubhouse. I remember this tall, lanky kid - he looked like he was 16 years old at the time. "This is the first round pick? *OK."* [Laughs] Little did we know what he was going to turn into.

TOM GORMAN: He was one of those guys where the other team would stick around for BP on the road, just to watch him hit. I think the first month of that season in '83 when he got called up, it was obvious who was going to be the Rookie of the Year.

MIKE TORREZ: Darryl had all the tools - he could run, he could throw, he could hit. There was nothing that he was lacking. He was great. In fact, they played a trick on him when he first came up. I always had my seat in the back of the plane - the very last seat - always, always in my career. And we were in the airport, but he had apparently gotten on the plane earlier than I did when we were boarding, and I guess some of the guys told him, "Go sit in that chair back there." When I came on the plane, I looked at him, and said, "Darryl, what are you doing?" He had his earphones on. I said, "What are you doing sitting here? This is *my seat* - get your ass up! Who told you to sit here?" "The guys!" "No!

This is my seat - they're messing with you. Get the hell out of my seat!" I said, "Darryl, once you get as many years as I've been in the big leagues, you can have this seat. But until I get out of here, that's my seat on the planes. Remember that!" [Laughs]

STEVE JACOBSON: I remember [Mets coach] Bill Robinson saying, "If this is the best we'll see from Darryl Strawberry, I'll be disappointed." Strawberry would take a "nap" in the outfield, and would be surprised by things that happened. I can't be a psychiatrist enough, but it was a mistake when he went to Los Angeles when he left the Mets [Strawberry played for the Dodgers from 1991-1993], because he had a cocoon...a comfort zone. Frank Cashen took personal interest in him and tried to help him along, and I'm not sure Strawberry appreciated that all the time. But he went to the Dodgers, and it didn't get better. He was back in "the hood," and that's not what he needed.

BRENT GAFF: You could see he had all the tools. I think he had a lot of pressure put on him. I would say he wasn't as good a teammate as Gooden was...I don't know, me and him kind of got into it a few times. But I think he had a lot of pressure put on him too early. That would be tough on anybody - he comes up and he's 20 years old or whatever he was when he first got to the big leagues [Strawberry was 21], and they expect him to hit third in the line-up and carry the team and all this. I thought he did a heck of a job handling the media and all that stuff. Because New York media just chewed me up and spit me out. After my major league debut, I was supposed to be "The Next Tom Seaver," and then a month later, the paper's saying, "What is this idiot doing in the big leagues?" It's either White House or Shit House in New York - it changes that fast.

STEVE JACOBSON: Hernandez always was pushing Strawberry to be better, and Strawberry resented it.

Strawberry, who once was late for spring training - an exhibition game - said his alarm clock broke. Another day in spring training that was picture day, Strawberry took a swing at Hernandez. For a long time, Strawberry acknowledged Hernandez as a mentor, and Hernandez was asking for more - for better - from Strawberry.

RICK OWNBEY: I was in the big leagues the first time I ever saw [Dwight Gooden] or met him, and they had brought him into New York, and he had come into the locker room. Y'know, #1 pick [in the 1982 draft], they're walking him around and introducing him. And back in the '80s, a lot of us were pitching around 88/90 miles an hour. I was a power pitcher, there were times I could get it to 92/93, and back then, that was bringing it pretty good. And obviously, the game's changed - a lot of people are throwing 95 and above.

But when Doc came in there, they were walking him around, and I remember a couple of the veteran players asked him about his pitches, and I heard somebody say, "So, just how hard do you throw?" And he said real easy, "Oh, *about 95 miles an hour."* We kind of chuckled a little bit, because, well, why stop there? Why not just call it 100? Because I don't think anybody in there threw 95, and at that time, you didn't really hear about 95. And the reason why I chuckle is because it was just a matter of time until we all figured out that he throws about 95. [Laughs]

BRENT GAFF: For some reason, it didn't look like he was that overpowering [when Gaff played with Gooden in the minor leagues], when you're sitting in the dugout, watching him. But he just kept throwing zeros up there on the board, and I'm thinking, "Well, this guy can't get any better. His curveball's nasty, his fastball locates, he's got a great changeup. He's really good, but I don't see how he could ever improve." And then he wins that Triple A game, that last game, so he won that World Series ring, and then in spring training in '84…back then, if you were wearing number 69 in spring training, your chances of making the club ain't that good. He had number 62 or 69 or one of them that you usually don't see, but I think Davey had to do a lot of talking to get him to stick with the team, and that's the year he broke all the records as a rookie.

But Goody was a good dude. I never knew anything about him ever doing drugs or anything like that, which I know later down the road he got in trouble doing that or something, but I never knew him like that. But thinking back on it, when he drives into major league camp and he's got a new Camaro and it says "DR. K" on it - maybe that had something to do with it. But I got along really good with Dwight. He was a really humble kid when he came up. And as far as I knew, I never heard anybody say anything bad about him. He was always friendly. He was a really good teammate.

CRAIG SWAN: I just remember Dwight coming - because he was from St. Pete - to the complex where we were in St. Pete, and gets out of the car, and gets his uniform on, and starts to throw some pitches on the side. And I'm like, "Holy moly, this guy's got some stuff! He's got a curveball that breaks two feet, and he throws mid-90's." I knew in spring training this kid was going to be really special - just from the stuff he had. He had a shortened career, but some good numbers.

CHARLIE PULEO: I remember coming up later on when I was in Cincinnati, and we faced him in New York. He was outstanding. Davey Concepción came back to the dugout and said he knew every pitch he was throwing - he was tipping his pitches. Well, when Gooden throws a three-hit shutout and strikes out twelve, it didn't really matter if you knew what was coming or not! He was *that talented*. And it showed early in his career.

MIKE TORREZ: Dwight was great. In fact, we were in spring training, and he came out to me in the field, he said to me, "Mike, the team is asking me if I would consider going to Triple A." Because they had to make a cut - they didn't know what to do with Dick Tidrow and Craig Swan. And I said, "Hell no! You go back in there and tell them you're ready to pitch in the big leagues. Look, you may take my job one of these days, but go back in there and tell them you're ready. You don't ever want to go to Triple A. *Go tell them you're ready to pitch in the big leagues."* So he did - he ran back in there and told them he wanted to stay with the big club.

TOM GORMAN: Darryl and Dwight both were very young. I think both of them were maybe 19 when they broke in [again, Darryl was 21 in 1983, and Dwight was 19 in 1984]. When I broke in, I was 23/24 - that's quite a difference in age. I remember Darryl hitting these mammoth shots. Not these ones that barely got out, it was monumental shots - as a rookie. They kind of used kid gloves with him - the media. And Doc too, where they kind of protected them, which I thought was a smart thing to do - early in their careers.

CHAPTER 21:
SEAVER

PAT ZACHRY: We could have, I suppose once or twice - but neither one of us wanted to talk about it [in response to being asked if he and Seaver ever discussed the infamous 1977 trade]. And I haven't seen him since. History will be his judge - I think he's going to be OK.

LENNY RANDLE: Tom had a little David Letterman in him, then he'd have some Leno in him one day, and the next day he's on the mound, he's like [MMA fighter] Randy Couture, or Mike Tyson, or Rocky! He had a multiple - on and off the field - personality. But was charismatic. It was jovial, and he knew when to put it on and turn it off. Because he kept us loose. He'd go, "I got this guy. Don't worry about it." He had a formula for getting guys out the day before. His pitching plan was different from whatever scouting report, because he had almost a photographic type memory - like a Bob Shapiro or Johnnie Cochran. He just had a photographic memory for getting guys out.

SKIP LOCKWOOD: Tom Seaver's a Hall of Famer. Not that I didn't play with Hall of Famers before - I played with Nolan Ryan in California. Tom was a kind of guy that would try to help you. A lot of the superstars are people that compete so hard themselves they don't have a lot of time to help other people. But I was just a kid coming along, Tom thought I threw well enough, that he wanted me to come in and save his games. So that made a big difference for me, having a guy like Tom say to me before the game, "Get your fat butt ready, because you're going to come in and try to save a game for me tonight if I come out."

Having his kind of confidence, he was a guy that was a deep guy. He knew a lot about a lot of different things - he knew a lot about wines. Tom was an interesting person just by himself. But he worked so hard, and he studied the game so much. He was able to challenge you to become better - just by preparation and by the things that he would say about hitters and the way you pitched and the way you approached the game. He really helped me to be better - not only physically, but emotionally. The way I went out to the mound, the way I'd try to pitch guys - curveballs and the selection of pitches. And of course, throwing to Jerry Grote was great during those years, too, because Jerry was a guy that took no quarter with anybody that wasn't going to go out there and prepare and be the best they could be. Tom Seaver was clearly - and still is - a friend, and a guy that really tried to help me. It was very evident with him.

CRAIG SWAN: We were both hard-throwing right-handers, and so basically, Tom would help me - if I could get next to him in the dugout during a game that we weren't pitching, then I would just keep asking him questions on what he would do in this situation with this hitter, and learning the hitters' weak spots and things like that. I learned a lot of that from Tom. That was a very important part of being able to pitch in the big leagues - you had to learn all the hitters and remember what pitch to throw in certain situations.

WALT TERRELL: Great teammate. Just to watch him and to be around him, and see the way he went about things, and how he did his "business," and just to listen to him - sitting in the dugout, "Hey did you see what he just did? He tipped his pitch. Make sure you're not doing this." Just his work ethic and the way he carried himself off the field. He was very good to me, and I'm very appreciative of that. Very much. I got to play a lot of pepper with him and talked about this and that. Was very fortunate to be around a Hall of Famer - you knew he was going to be, it was just a matter of time at that point.

MIKE FITZGERALD: I was catching a baseball legend. And I was catching someone that personally I thought we had four or five guys in Triple A that were throwing better stuff than he threw that day at Shea. I was smart enough to know though that he was not only a very confident guy, but he'd been a winner his whole life, and a great Met. I did the best I could and things didn't go that well that day at Shea - I remember it was a day game [the game Fitzgerald is referencing was probably the one on September 14, 1983, which the Mets lost, 2-1, to the St. Louis Cardinals at Shea].

But catching him, I don't know, I felt I should be able to get a win out of whoever I caught - that's the way I always thought about it. If I didn't, I took responsibility for that personally. But Tom, he ended up leaving and pitching pretty well for a few more years [after leaving the Mets again after 1983, Seaver pitched for the Chicago White Sox from 1984-1986 and the Boston Red Sox in 1986]. But I believe that was the only game I caught him, and really didn't think much of it at the time - other than, "OK. Tom's my pitcher today and he's a veteran, so I'm just going to do my best to call the right pitches that he would want to throw, and go a good job for him."

MIKE TORREZ: We were both probably towards the ends of our careers. Very competitive. He and I, we knew what our jobs were and we went about it and did it. That's why we always were successful - we never gave in to hitters, that's one of the main things that I can remember. He went about it, and he was an aggressive pitcher. I patterned myself a little bit - going after hitters and throw strikes. That was the most important thing - to get ahead of the count.

STEVE JACOBSON: He was expected to be the "Keith Hernandez of the pitching staff," and it turned out to be not the case. He didn't go out of his way to help other people - to teach or to mentor other people. He had all this wisdom, he was such a brilliant pitcher, and he was much more into himself at that time.

MIKE TORREZ: Tom was a little bit tough to communicate with at times. A lot of times, you couldn't really read him. He was kind of quiet. He was a type of person where you could see a lot of things, he didn't like to be bothered with - put it that way. [Laughs]

CRAIG SWAN: Oh, he was great with me. We were good friends. I moved up to Connecticut in 1980, and so for years during the off-season, a lot of squash, a lot of golf - until the snow came. We palled around for years up there. He was a good friend. I know he's sometimes put off by other people, only because I think there were so many requests coming in. People wanted him to do something about this charity and that charity, and he did a lot of that work, but he tried to stay somewhat separate I think from a certain part of the fame, I think.

PAT ZACHRY: Well, those years in the late '70s/early '80s, were not real good for the Mets. But hell, with Seaver, Koosman, and Matlack, those guys were winning 20 games a year, anyway. So it may or may not have made a big difference - who knows [in response to being asked about Craig Swan's earlier comment, that he wasn't sure if Seaver would have reached 300 career wins if he remained with the Mets]. History's always 20/20, ain't it? Those three guys were as good as it comes, and you don't run into many years of mediocre numbers with Tom Seaver, so I know he was my idol in that period of time. He was one of the guys that I looked up to.

SKIP LOCKWOOD: He's the best pitcher I ever saw. I mean, as far as pitching goes and throwing, throwing hard, throwing strikes, and pitching the plate, pitching to hitters, I thought Tom was the best I'd ever seen.

CHAPTER 22:
OTHER METS

~~Neil Allen~~

JEFF REARDON: I actually took Neil's place in Lynchburg, Virginia, with my first team in A Ball. I was going to be sent to Little Falls, and I was like their "low rookie." And Neil had just gotten mononucleosis. So in the transition of them signing me, all of a sudden, they said, "No, no. You're going to go to Lynchburg to take over for a guy named Neil Allen." So that actually helped me, because I had a little temper in baseball, and somebody said, "The coach of Little Falls, I don't think he would have put up with your shit." [Laughs] I'm kind of lucky, because the guy was a real hard ass, you had to do everything his way. I just took the game really hard, and had a temper.

And then the next year, I saw Neil in spring training. The thing that impressed me about him the most was his curveball. A lot of people have a good curveball, but his was like, *over the top*. Almost a drop straight down. That's how teams wanted a curveball. Anybody can throw a slurve or a slider, but the one that's coming in with that 12-6 spin, I was impressed. Plus, he got it up there in the low 90's, but the thing I had over him was I had better control than him. Because he could get himself in trouble and he seemed to get hit more than me. I knew as long as he was there, I wasn't going to be the closer, because he was their "next Lee Mazzilli" - the way they treated Mazzilli, like the bonus baby. But a great guy. I had good friends on that team.

PETE FALCONE: Neil came up in 1979 with us. As a

matter of fact, we roomed together for a while. And he just had good, raw stuff. He was young, he was happy to be there, and then he established himself. They put him in the bullpen as a closer, and I think that's really where his career took off. That was a good move by Joe Torre at the time, when he did that. That was a good move for Neil. Now, I understand Neil is a pitching coach for the Minnesota Twins.

JOHN STEARNS: Neil came up, he was a two-pitch pitcher. A young kid. Had a great arm. Fastball, curveball. I think we got him into the closer's role a little too soon. But I liked Neil and I thought Neil was aggressive on the mound and just got out there and threw two-plus pitches. That's all he had. He was just a thrower, and he was feeding them a fastball, curveball - a great curveball. As it turned out, he got hit quite a bit at times. As far as him being a closer, that was a little above his area where he felt comfortable. He didn't have great control or command when he was with us, anyway.

PAT ZACHRY: Threw a really good fastball - much like the same as Mike Scott, but had that 12-6 curveball that was just unreal. I was surprised when he started as a relief pitcher - whoever's idea that was, was a good one, because he made a great short man for the Mets and some other teams.

WALT TERRELL: Great teammate, funny guy. Electric stuff off the mound. Boy, he threw hard, had a great breaking ball. Very competitive guy. Back then, he was used as a closer, and then he went to St. Louis and I think he did some starting there. But lights out - very electric stuff. Glad to have been a teammate of that young man.

RICK OWNBEY: I definitely spent some time with Neil, too. Good guy, and he was getting it done at that time. He was basically the closer coming out of the pen and he did his job pretty well. I got along with Neil really good, and then we got traded and went to Triple A, so I split away from him a little bit, but then made the Cardinal team, and we were teammates again.

~~Wally Backman~~

GARY "BABA BOOEY" DELL'ABATE: Just being one of those faceless little guys that just was really tough. Sort of like Lenny Dykstra. Dykstra you remember from the day he got there. He always appeared to me to be one of those guys to be working way too hard. There are a lot of comparisons to Pete Rose, and I think they were pretty good. He was one of those guys that seemed to work harder than he had to - because he wanted to, because it meant that much to him.

JOHN STEARNS: Wally was a little guy, he was a grinder - a good, little hitter. Not a very good second baseman, but OK - adequate out there. Just a hard-nosed kid that played the game well. He could hit. He knew the strike zone and a line drive hitter to all fields. He ended up having a pretty good career. #1 draft pick [in 1977]. When you first saw him, you thought, "How did he go in the first round?" He was a little, short, stumpy guy, right? He'd spray the ball around though and he could hit. But limited at second base defensively.

PETE FALCONE: He was a crafty, gutty player. Wally Backman...what was he, 5'9"? But I'll tell you what, when he played baseball, he was out there, he'd get dirty every night. Wally Backman was a gamer. He was a warrior out there.

RICK OWNBEY: That was one tough cookie. Wally was one tough competitor. Not afraid to get dirty. Gave you

110%, played as hard as can be, and a tremendous teammate. When I think of Wally, it just felt like he always had my back. If there was going to be a confrontation at the mound, obviously, your first baseman or third baseman [were located closest to the pitcher], but Wally was going to stick his head right in there. He made you feel quite secure and what a great teammate and what a great competitor he was.

WALT TERRELL: I was fortunate enough to play with him in the big leagues and minor leagues, and kept in touch with him once in a while since then. What a "table setter" kind of guy. Boy, how competitive was he? He didn't want to beat you 3-0. "Let's beat the hell out of them - let's beat them *10-0* if we can." Always energetic and happy. But a very competitive guy. Fun to be around, a guy you wanted as a teammate.

JEFF REARDON: I'm just praying he gets a chance to manage the Mets. Me and him were really good friends. We got to come up a little together, played in the big leagues together, came to Minnesota, we kept in touch over the years. Nothing against the manager that they have [Terry Collins], but Wally...I told Wilpon once, I went to something Carter had, and the son was there, Jeff. I said, "Hey, *Wally's your man.* I'm telling you, if you want to have a winner..." And that Collins guy was right behind me! Jeff goes, "Hey, keep it down." Of course, I didn't know who the hell it was. [Laughs] He's just a tough guy - I respect Wally a lot. He's a gamer. I think if you translate him into a manager, he's the one that could "bring them back." Wally, he's got a temper, and nowadays, the guys need that. They don't take the game as hard as we did, I don't think.

~~Bruce Bochy~~

JOHN STEARNS: I remember him, and he was in spring training with us. I think he might have come north a little bit. He was a big guy - not a quick, fast guy. Pretty good catcher - just a quiet individual. Kind of a really intelligent, smooth, low-key type of guy. Kind of perfect for what he's doing now, which is managing [the San Francisco Giants, who at the time of this book's release, has led the team to three World Series Championships - 2010, 2012, and 2014]. He had the perfect mindset, the perfect personality. He was the exact opposite of me - I was more loud and aggressive, and he was more conservative and didn't say too much. A smart guy, and fun to be around. But kind of just lurked around in the background. He didn't have a prominent position as a player on our team, so he kind of took his back-up catching job and went that way. But that was fine. I can see where he's having great success as a manager. I can see where his personality and demeanor is great with the players of today.

BRENT GAFF: I never even thought about that stuff [if Gaff had any idea that Bochy had the makings of a great major league manager]. I knew some of the guys that were interested, like, me and Rick Anderson were always good buddies. He was a pitching coach [for the Minnesota Twins]. But anytime I was working down in the bullpen, Andy was always there watching, and so was I - I paid attention. And Gardenhire was always asking me questions - "Gaffer, why in the hell didn't we bunt? Why didn't we do this and that?" And I'm like, "Hell, I don't know. Davey's got a hunch. I don't know what he's doing." Gardy was always wondering why Davey wasn't going to bunt. Well, Davey was trained by Earl Weaver, and Weaver played for a big inning, and that's what Davey did. Y'know, bunt and play small ball - this college crap.

But Boch, I just listened to him. The first game I threw in Triple A was to him, and it was against Pawtucket [Red Sox] - it was Wade Boggs and all those guys. And I had a three-hit shutout into the ninth inning, and I used to kind of "style it" on the last pitch of the game, and drop down - even if it was to a left-hander - I would drop down and throw a big, swooping, 60 mile an hour sidearm curveball, that would just float up there like a Frisbee. And that's how I'd end the game. I did it maybe half a dozen times to end the ballgame for strike three calls, because I never threw it except for the last pitch of the game. And Bochy called for a changeup, and that's what I threw. There was a guy on third base. It was a called third strike and he missed it, and the runner scored from third!

But I can remember that first time I came up, the very first pitch I threw, he was behind the plate in Triple A. Like I said, it was in Pawtucket, and the first pitch I threw - because I had to keep the ball down or I'd get shelled - a fastball right down the middle, knee-high, with a sink on it, and he called it a ball. Well, after that inning, I walked up the umpire, and I said, "Hey man, if that first pitch I threw is a ball, *I'm going to get shelled.* I'm going to get my tits lit, because I can't live upstairs." And Bochy grabbed a hold of me and said, "You just leave them alone. I'll take care of this." He took command - he knew what he wanted his pitchers to do.

He was a good dude. He was my catcher in Venezuela - we kind of hung out. He stayed at our house, because his wife was never with him, and it's usually just me and my wife, and he'd stay with us a lot of times. On the road, we hung out together. But yeah, Boch was smart, but he never really said a whole lot. He really didn't talk a whole lot. You could tell his wheels were always turning. He was a really smart catcher, but you could say they were always grooming somebody else, and I think that kind of ticked him off. Because he was always a back-up catcher, kinda. He really wasn't very happy about that, because they were always bringing some young punk up that was going to get a shot, and he may not. But as far as him being [a manager], it doesn't surprise me, because I knew how smart he was.

~~Hubie Brooks~~

TOM GORMAN: Hube was one of the greatest guys I ever played with, when it came to being just a neat guy. I really, really loved that guy. I don't think anybody would have a bad word to say about that guy. He treated everybody nice. I thought he was a fantastic player. But his trade brought Gary over. Gary was the first catcher I ever threw to in the big leagues, and then to play the '85 season with him was great. I think the best story about Gary was opening day, I was playing cards and Davey came by, and I said, "Skip, I'm going to get the win this day, 6-5 in the 11th." Doc was starting the game, so he goes, "Fax, if you *sniff* this game, I'll be surprised." Anyway, I come in - 5-5 in the 10th! I come in, get out of it, Gary hits a home run in the bottom of the 10th...6-5, we win in the 10th. I missed it by one inning. That was always a big deal - that I had "called the shot," or whatever. Hube to leave was tough, he was a great guy.

JEFF REARDON: They were high on him. Hubie was another great guy. I felt he was a tad slow for third base, but he could hit. He had some power. And then he ended up coming up to Montreal a couple of years later with me, and he played third base for us up there. He was a gamer - he gave you 100%.

JOHN STEARNS: Hubie came up, he showed a lot of potential. Hubie, he had a different type of personality. He wasn't real hard-nosed or aggressive. In a game for him, he was laughing a lot, he was low-key. Kind of the opposite of me, where I was into every game and going 110 miles an hour. I think Hubie kind of relaxed. And then when he got out of New York, I think he settled in and started really playing some good baseball with the Expos. He struggled with the Mets - it was tough for him, for a couple of years. And then when he left, I think he found out how to be a big leaguer, and he became a good player. He had the ability, but when he was with us, it was a struggle. I just thought he could have approached the game better. I thought he was too light-hearted and laughing and joking when he was on the field. When he left, he got better at that, and became a good player.

MIKE TORREZ: Hubie, at that time, he didn't have that good of a year - the first year I was with him [1983]. He struggled a little bit. He just needed a little bit of talking to him, assuring him, "Hey, you're going to make mistakes, so just learn from them." But it kind of ate him up a little bit. We had to kind of nourish him a little bit and pat him on the back, and say, "You know what? Shit's going to happen over there in the hot spot. Don't let it bother you, don't let it eat you up."

PETE FALCONE: He played third base for the National League as a rookie - *come on!* And he did the best job he could do. I have nothing bad to say about Hubie Brooks. He was young at the time, and they expected a lot of him. He was a good prospect. He played third base and it is a tough place to play in the National League, and I'm sure it is in any time in the major leagues. And he did boot a lot of balls. He did. But it wasn't like he wasn't trying. He had earned his position there. There was nobody to replace him with, and they put him out there to get his brains beat in. What's wrong with that? But he hit the ball pretty good. He didn't have to worry about being the guy that they had to zero in on. Kingman hit behind him if I remember correctly, or George - he didn't have to worry about that. Hubie was a good player. A solid player.

WALT TERRELL: He did very well when I was there. Very good glove, great arm, was hitting home runs and a good guy. Kept you positive if you were on the mound and struggling - "Hell, have them hit one to me. I'll get us out of this damn thing." Always fun to be around, always had a smile on his face, and always busted his ass to get better. A good person.

RICK OWNBEY: Hubie Brooks I thought was a tremendous player and a tremendous teammate. If I'm not wrong, Hubie was from California [Los Angeles]. He did everything he could to really make me feel comfortable. Anything he could do - from advice…and again, he was at third base and you're on the pitcher's mound, obviously, there's quite a bit of contact with your third baseman. He's going to give you that last toss, normally the flip, or come in and talk to you.

BOBBY VALENTINE: I remember Hubie's great smile, his caring attitude, his ability to hit the ball to the opposite field. Hubie was another really good player on a team that really wasn't up to his capabilities at the time. He could really get a hit.

~~Ron Darling~~

STEVE JACOBSON: I recall Cashen traded for two pitchers from Texas, and one of them was Ron Darling [along with Walt Terrell, for Lee Mazzilli, on April 1, 1982], who was quite a good pitcher. And he's a pretty good broadcaster. And Terrell, I think he had one decent year with them. I don't think he had more than that.

MIKE TORREZ: Ron was an outstanding pitcher in the major leagues. I talked to him a lot and took him under my wing - him and Dwight Gooden. And told him he had to be mentally tough - especially every day, there's going to be a grind. There's no "give me's" or nothing. You've got to battle every time you hit that mound. Get yourself mentally prepared and go get 'em.

STEVE JACOBSON: Very gutty pitcher. Very smart. Good interview and a pitcher with a lot of talent. He was on the cover of...I believe it was GQ, for men's fashion. And Bobby Ojeda's comment on seeing that was, *"I can be there. I can wear beige."* Darling was a very elegant dresser.

~~Doug Flynn~~

JEFF REARDON: Doug Flynn was - up to that point - the best second baseman I ever saw play. Probably even to this day, I never had a second baseman as good as him. And another thing I remember about him, he was very nice to me coming up. I don't know if it was because we had the same agent, but he treated me with a lot of respect and tried to get me used to being comfortable. I always appreciated that with him - I told him years later, when he ended up going to Montreal for a little while. And a very nice guy.

PETE FALCONE: Doug Flynn was not much of a hitter - I think he'd even tell you that. But he could pick it. And [Flynn's 1980 Gold Glove Award] was rightly deserved. For a guy to win a Gold Glove on a last place team [actually second to last], that says something. And he did a good job. He had good range, he was a good guy...we had some bright spots.

DAN NORMAN: He was doing a good job - I know he was playing good defense. He was playing second base, and we also played together with Montreal, too. So we still remain friends to this day.

PAT ZACHRY: Best fielding glove guy that I was ever with. Bar none.

~~Brent Gaff~~

MIKE FITZGERALD: He probably didn't tell you, but he was pitching with a sore arm in the big leagues. It probably happened in Triple A, where it started to go on him. But he's pretty tough and he wasn't afraid to throw strikes to anybody. And he had a good sinker and a cutter before guys were throwing cutters, kind of. A good curveball, and a nice little change. If he hadn't of hurt his arm, he'd be still traveling every winter to New York, doing autograph sessions. There's a lot of players that get hurt, people don't know - they just know, "Oh, what's his average?" or "How many wins did he get?" They don't know what's really going on with some players as far as their health and what's happening.

~~Ron Gardenhire~~

CHARLIE PULEO: Gardy was a hard-nosed kid. He came up out of the University of Texas [at Austin], and had a great career in college. Excellent defensive player. And he could handle the bat pretty good. I guess he ended up studying the game pretty well, because he turned into a pretty good manager [who managed the Minnesota Twins from 2002-2014, and was named "AL Manager of the Year" in 2010]. He had a heck of a career as a manager, and brought Rick Anderson along with him - he's an old New York Met farmhand, too, who had a great career as a pitching coach. So he did very well, and he was an important part of those early '80s Mets teams, too.

~~Ron Hodges~~

JEFF REARDON: I really liked Hodges - he caught me in the bullpen most of the time, because he didn't start that much. He would help me with suggestions more than any of the other ones. Alex Treviño was a little younger than me, but Hodges would always seem to work with me in the bullpen as I was getting ready for a game. He'd remind me, "Do this, do that." I looked up to Hodges and I listened to him. He caught me more than Stearns, because he was always catching in the bullpen. But Treviño was great to throw to. He was an all-around catcher - he could hit, his defense I thought was amazing, he was quick throwing people out. So I'd rate him probably the best defensive catcher.

~~Randy Jones~~

CHARLIE PULEO: I think Randy got off to a really good start in '82, but he was a little older at the time, and injuries started catching up with him down the road. But he was great. I've never seen anybody chew tobacco like he did - I think there was one incident where he spit on Craig Swan, and Craig was chasing him around the whole warning track! That was back in the day when a lot of people were chewing tobacco and spitting it all over the place. He was notorious for taking care of the rookies and making sure their shoes were full of tobacco chew. Randy was funny - he was a comedian and he also had an outstanding career. I think he got to New York a little late. But what he did in San Diego was unbelievable.

~~Ed Kranepool~~

JEFF REARDON: He was a very quiet guy. He never said that much. The Mets were pretty much using him for pinch-hitting and playing first once in a while. I thought he was a nice guy - he wasn't cocky or anything, compared to a lot of players that tend to be cocky.

~~Jesse Orosco~~

JOHN STEARNS: He came up to the majors quickly, and stayed a long time [24 seasons, from 1979, 1981-2003]. He's the kind of lefty that lefties can't touch, because his breaking ball was phenomenal. The best curveball I've seen almost from any pitcher. Just a big, deep, 45-degree angle. Big, hard breaking ball. Against lefties, you'd bring him in - they had no chance of hitting his breaking ball. He was impressive.

JEFF REARDON: Me and him were good friends. He's a guy that could pitch every day. I know at the end, he didn't have to pitch a whole lot of innings, but no closers do at the end. But he would go three or four innings in middle relief, and would be ready to go the next day. That's the way it was back then. Another one that was a gamer. I remember his big, sweeping curveball, and for a lefty, he got it up there pretty good. A little over 90. With that curveball, lefties did not   like   hitting   off   him   at   all.

RICK OWNBEY: I actually lived with Jesse and Scott Holman - at one point, we were all in one house. Jesse, just amazing to me how long he ended up playing. And boy, at that time, he was one tough left-hander, on getting an inning or an out. Just the way he handled himself on the mound. Tremendous ballplayer, tremendous guy. High kudos for Jesse.

CHARLIE PULEO: Jesse always had a lot of talent - you saw that in Triple A. A left-hander and had a real live fastball. He had a real sharp breaking ball. You knew he was going to be real tough on left-handed hitters and would have a great career - and he did. We were roommates for a while - that first year. I think it was him that was snoring too much, so we had to make sure we ended that real quick!

But he might have been my first roommate in the big leagues. Jesse was a big talent and it showed down the road.

WALT TERRELL: He's a worthless piece of shit...just kidding! [Laughs] No, we hung around - so good for Jesse and his family. The guy worked hard, and had been in the big leagues for a while, but had some success - but not over the top success. And finally gets that closer's role, and really does a tremendous job for a long time. I know he was very good to the organization for the years that he put in and how well he had done. Just a good person - a very good person. Always smiling, laughing, and cutting up. Pleasure to have been a teammate.

MIKE TORREZ: Jesse was coming into his own. He became even better after I left. He had a great arm, and he was the kind of a kid that was not scared to go out there and pitch. He'd get the ball and he'd challenge you. Jesse knew how to get you out. He never gave into anybody - not when I was there, and not when I saw him after my career, when I'd see him on TV. He was that kind of a pitcher, where he was a battler and was not scared of anything. He enjoyed playing, and enjoyed his beers - he was one of the few kids that could drink his beer pretty good...and chew tobacco at the same time!

~~Jeff Reardon~~

PETE FALCONE: Jeff Reardon, when you first saw him, the way he threw - "This guy's got a great arm." When he went out there, he was confident, he wanted the ball every night. He was like, "Give me the ball. *I want the ball.* Not you." He was competing at the time with Neil Allen, and Neil was a good reliever, too. Neil had good stuff - hard curveball. I just guess it was too crowded in the bullpen back then for all that talent, so they had to make some changes. Jeff went to the Expos from there. Jeff had a great career.

JEFF REARDON: I don't know why they traded me - I'll never understand that. Frank Cashen said it was the worst trade he ever made in his career - which I believe it was, too. See, they were really high on Neil Allen, because he was their "bonus baby," and I think that's the only difference. Neil was good, but I always felt I was better. And I kind of proved that. So Torre, I don't think it was him that traded me. I think it was Cashen, after hearing that Cashen said that.

They just called me in after the game, and said, "We traded you to Montreal - you and Dan Norman for Ellis Valentine. I just want to wish you good luck." I think it was Cashen who told me. I said, "Alright. Thank you." And that was it. Otherwise, I'd have been on the mound and maybe not Orosco in '86, because I was always well ahead of him as a closer. I mean, he ended up with a great career - don't get me wrong - but I was more of a closer. He wasn't even a name yet in New York. But I was happy for him when he saved that game [Game 7 of the 1986 World Series], because the following year, I got the save for Minnesota [when the Twins beat the Cardinals in Game 7 of the 1987 World Series]. So, two years in a row, me and Jesse. We palled together, we came up together in the minors - me, Jesse, and Neil Allen. It was three good relievers they had.

~~Mike Scott~~

DAN NORMAN: When we were in Triple A, I thought that he threw hard, I thought he threw well. I didn't think he had much movement on his ball, at the time. But he was a horse out there. When he got to Houston, his coach was Roger Craig, and he taught him how to get more movement on the ball. And he really took off.

PETE FALCONE: I remember Mike Scott in spring training. I remember he was just a right hand pitcher with a good arm - fastball, curveball. Good stuff, the ball moved good. A right-hander in the National League then and now - who could throw the ball around 90/91 miles an hour with a curveball - is ho-hum. What's the big deal? And Mike didn't have dynamic stuff. He had good stuff. He was a big league pitcher, what can you say? But he had a good attitude. See, I remember Mike's attitude...if Mike got beat up in a game, he was the same person as if he pitched nine innings and threw a shutout. And he had that attitude...it was an "I don't care attitude," I think he had a self-confidence that he'd laugh a lot and he was a good guy.

I remember when he went to the Astros - as a matter of fact, I was on the Braves when he went to the Astros. And one night, Mike Scott comes out and pitches against us. We had a good team, and he overmatched us. And I said to myself, "Hmm, this isn't the same Mike Scott that I remember." Because he started playing with a forkball, and then they said he was cheating a little bit [many accused Scott of scuffing baseballs]. Maybe he was - I believe he was, a little bit. But he turned it around, he really turned it around. I think Roger Craig taught him that [a split-fingered fastball] in Houston. That thing like, *broke off a table.* But he was a guy that went out there loose as a goose, was confident, and nothing bothered him. And he was also a really good golfer!

CRAIG SWAN: It was simple - he had good stuff, he had a hard fastball and a pretty good slider, but when he got traded, Roger Craig taught him the split-fingered fastball. And as soon as he learned the split-fingered fastball, he was an All-Star [in 1986, 1987, and 1989, as well as winning the NL Cy Young Award in '86]. He was going to be a good pitcher, but not an All-Star - until he learned that pitch. Then he became just a devastating pitcher.

PAT ZACHRY: When I knew him, he could hardly throw a breaking ball. He had kind of a curveball and a "slurve" or whatever you want to call it. And then all of a sudden, somebody taught him how to throw a split-finger, and you couldn't touch him. I mean, hell, the guy threw 95+ most of the time, and he could throw forever. He had big old horse legs - a big, strong California kid. He had a good, rising, moving fastball. But when he learned how to throw something that would break off the table like that split-finger did, it was a totally different ballgame. He didn't have to be second fiddle to anybody after that.

JOHN STEARNS: He came up and I was catching him, and he threw hard. He had a little cut slider. He was a hard throwing pitcher and a lot of movement on the ball. Sometimes, he was really hard to catch, because you'd call a fastball, and sometimes he would put a cut on it, and it would run a little bit like a slider. Other times, he'd throw a nasty sinker. And he's throwing like, 93/94. Really, a tough guy to catch for me, because I didn't know which way his fastball was going to move. He lacked any kind of off-speed pitch at that time - he just threw a hard fastball, a hard slider. I think that's why he struggled with us.

And then later on, he went down and had a lot of success with the Astros. I think he learned a lot more about how to pitch. When he came up with us, he was just "a thrower," with a great arm. And when he went down to the Astros, he started to move the ball around, change speeds a little bit, go upstairs, come back down, inside, outside - he learned how to pitch. And of course, he had a tremendous body and arm, and became a star. It didn't surprise me. But we only had him, what, one or two years? [Scott was with the Mets from 1979-1982] He got knocked around good, even though he had a great arm. Tough to catch and he needed an off-speed pitch. I think he found that after he left.

BRENT GAFF: Mike was a really nice guy. He was a good guy. I don't think he was doing any backstabbing or anything like that. He had really good stuff - he just needed that forkball. But he kept to himself - he was a quiet kind of guy. He wasn't really one to go out to the bars or do anything like that. He was pretty straight-laced in going about his business - him and Puleo both were like that.

RANDY JONES: For one thing, he had a great arm. I thought he was a thrower. He didn't know how to pitch real well when he was younger with the Mets. He'd go out there and boy, he had a great arm and threw well, but he just didn't know how to pitch and change speeds. I think we all know what the splitter did for him. But also, I just think the years of maturity - where he finally grew up and learned how to pitch - that's when he started being a great pitcher and chewing up innings. He was always big and strong, and I think he had a bit of that mentality - if he got in a jam, he'd throw a little bit harder. And then after a while, after he matured a little bit, he learned how to pitch, change speeds a little more, use his split finger, and that's when he really became effective and finally got the confidence I think you need at the big league level to be successful. And he did so.

WALT TERRELL: Very happy that he had the success that he did once he had left. I don't think he really wanted to leave, but very happy for him. Mike wasn't one of those guys when he got called up that wouldn't talk to you - he was very positive and helpful with hints and how to pitch certain guys or what to do. Just thoroughly enjoyed being around him, sitting on the bench talking to him, or whatever it might have been. Like I said, good person and very happy for the success he had once he did leave.

~~Doug Sisk~~

WALT TERRELL: Yeah, he's more worthless than

Orosco...no, good teammate! We roomed together for a while, and Doug had some success there. I'm happy for him. We were roommates, so a lot of BS back and forth, here and there, but always pulling for everybody on the team. A funny guy and the reason why I don't drink wine today - nah, just kidding! Very much a good person and glad for his success.

~~Rusty Staub~~

TOM GORMAN: Rusty was a veteran at the time. Let's put it this way, he invited us out to his restaurant [Rusty's] there on 73rd and 3rd, and we'd go there with the wives and there was probably six of us. So, twelve with the wives. And he shows up and gives us wine at the table, blah blah blah, and when it came to pay the check, there was no check. I was lucky enough to see him tie the record for hits in a row as a pinch hitter [in 1983, Staub tied the record set by Philadelphia's Dave Philley set in 1958, when he racked up eight consecutive pinch hits, from June 11th-June 26th]. And Rusty wasn't exactly the most "in-shape guy" you'd ever run into, y'know? I think he spent more time on the training table getting his back rubbed then he ever did hitting! But he treated everybody pretty good. I played cards with him all the time. I didn't have any bad feelings about Rusty.

CHARLIE PULEO: Rusty was a little quirky. With us at that time, he was pinch-hitting a lot. He played a little right field every once in a while - maybe a little first base. But he was mostly pinch-hitting. The only thing I remember is he was always in the training room, getting his feet rubbed or his back rubbed or his knees - *something* being rubbed. And he'd pop right out and get a base hit. He was one of the veterans on the club - along with guys like John Stearns and Randy Jones. They really were in charge of the clubhouse, and great to all the young guys.

JEFF REARDON: Just seeing him get his feet rubbed every game. The trainers, they'd rub his feet with some...I don't know, it looked disgusting - like something orange. I was like, *"What the hell?"* But you're not going to say nothing to Rusty, and I'd ask the trainers, and they'd say, "He needs a foot massage. He's a little older." He was actually pretty nice for such a veteran. Like I said, Kingman wasn't very nice, Staub was just the opposite.

~~Bobby Valentine~~

JOHN STEARNS: As a teammate, what surprised me the most was his injury - he really couldn't run without a limp [while playing for the California Angels on May 17, 1973, Valentine suffered a multiple compound leg fracture while playing the outfield]. He came over and had a bump in his leg, and was trying to play and was limping. He was supposed to have been really fast when he came up, but we couldn't see any of that because of the leg. It was surprising that he was not able to play I'm sure up to his capabilities when he came over. I just remember him as being a hardnosed guy, and just a great guy for the team, and trying to help everybody. It was sad that he probably couldn't play up to his level of expertise.

DAN NORMAN: I never thought about him being a manager at the time. But I'm glad he did. Nice person, good guy. I remember seeing him play and I remember when he broke his leg. That really hampered him. Those guys were older than me at the time, but I used to watch him play when he was with the Dodgers. He could run, throw, play many positions - until he broke his leg, when he was traded to the Angels.

GARY "BABA BOOEY" DELL'ABATE: I don't remember him a lot, except being a name that never lived up to the hype. And then years later, I really got to read a lot about it - that he was an amazing athlete that never quite got to play at 100% because of injuries. I remember him playing just as a name, but I don't have any vivid memories of, "Oh, he did something on this day or that day."

WALT TERRELL: A workaholic. Non-stop. Wanting to do something for somebody to make them better. "You need some extra hitting? Ground balls?" Even as a pitcher, he took me in extra to throw me bunting and those kinds of things. I thought Bobby was tremendous. Absolutely. Good baseball guy, good person, treated me extremely well. Was happy to see he got a job managing in the big leagues and was something I knew he would be very, very good at, because he was a non-stop working guy. A very positive human being. Good to be around for us younger players. Glad to have been on a team that he was coaching.

BRENT GAFF: You could always tell Bobby had high aspirations - in anything he did. He was always very confident. He liked me for some reason. He told me he liked me because I could throw it at different arm angles - I could throw sidearm or three-quarters or whatever. And he said, "Gaffer, you can pitch for me any day." But I had no idea he was trying to be a manager. I always respected him as a coach, because he always had interesting things to say. His career got cheated by that knee, because he probably would have been really a special player I would imagine, from what I heard about him. He was a strange guy though - Bobby just marched to the beat of a different drummer. He was really intelligent, I think. Some guys, like Billy Beane, it's hard to talk to some of those guys that are so smart.

JOHN STEARNS: Bobby was really smart - not only a really good baseball guy, but an exceptionally smart individual. I'm not surprised at all that he was a Major League manager with success. That was probably a given.

Bobby's a great baseball guy, very enthusiastic, positive person, and was a great manager.

~~Ellis Valentine~~

JOHN STEARNS: When he came down to us, it wasn't that he was fat, but he had put on some weight. When he came up [with the Montreal Expos], he looked like Superman. He had one of the best bodies I'd ever seen - he was 6'4" and had a skinny waist, long, strong arms and legs. He just looked like a physical freak out there. And he had the tools - the best tools you've ever seen on a baseball field, in terms of being able to run, his size, and his arm. The best arm I had ever seen in any player was on Ellis Valentine. He could throw a ball from the fence in right field - on the line - all the way to third base on the fly. It was ridiculous.

He and Andre Dawson came up almost at the same time, and Andre was the Hall of Famer. He didn't have anything on Ellis - Ellis was "the guy" everybody was looking at, not Andre. Ellis had more raw talent than Andre Dawson when they first came up at age 21 or whatever it was. And then, it didn't work out for him as well. But he was an exciting young player, with a lot of ability. And somehow, his mental approach held him back - that's all I want to say about that. There were things that he did that you just don't do and keep being a star. And then, by the time he was 30, he was putting weight on. I mean, this guy had the greatest body you'd ever seen at age 22. He really caught your eye. Even as a big leaguer, I'd never seen a big leaguer with that kind of ability. But it didn't pan out for him.

PETE FALCONE: You know what it was for these guys? It was a letdown, because they didn't have those guys around them - he didn't have Andre Dawson, he didn't have Warren Cromartie, he didn't have Gary Carter, to push them. There was nobody to really push them. See, like with the Expos, Ellis Valentine wasn't the only person on the team that they could look to. You had *six guys* in the line-up that could hit home runs and drive in a hundred RBI's. When he came to New York, he was the only guy that they depended on to do that. That put a lot of pressure on him. And he just couldn't cash in with the talent. The talent on the team just wasn't there. So I think that is why he didn't perform the way he should have performed. And one of the best arms in the outfield ever in the game.

~~Mookie Wilson~~

STEVE JACOBSON: A charmer. And he did a lot of things - he gave them some speed, which they didn't have. He stole bases. He was a good player. Everybody liked him, and he was also an energy producer. The team that became good - and should have won more than one championship - was an "energy team," that other teams in the league disliked. They did not like the Mets - they wanted to beat the Mets. And the Mets became good.

JEFF REARDON: Me and Mookie go all the way back to Jackson, Mississippi, too. He got married at home plate, while we were holding the bats up, with the uniforms on! Just one of the best center fielders I ever played with. He could run, he could switch-hit. He pretty much took up switch-hitting in the minors - I saw him transform, first as a right hand hitter. So that helped him a lot. He probably did that because of his speed. But another gamer. I was glad for him in '86, too.

JOHN STEARNS: Mookie caught your eye as soon as he came up. He came up and of course, he was the fastest guy around. He could steal bases and was a pretty good hitter. He ended up having a decent career. A pretty good hitter and as a center fielder, covered ground. Part of the '86 Mets, of course. You had to keep your eye on him, because he's going when he gets on first base. Not too many guys could run as good as Mookie. Offensively, his hitting was not as impressive as maybe his baserunning, but he tried to put the ball in play. A switch hitter.

PETE FALCONE: Mookie, another bright spot. One of the fastest guys I've ever seen. Man, he was *fast*. Mookie was dynamic. One of the things that I remember about Mookie is he led off with us, but he wasn't much of a bunter. If he learned how to bunt and drag a bunt, he'd have added   a   hundred   hits   a   year.

WALT TERRELL: Great person. He had great years with the Mets. What a class act. Just a tremendous person. Fun to watch him hit a triple - he could absolutely pick 'em up and put 'em down. Just fun to watch when you weren't playing, but boy, you were sure happy that he was in centerfield when you were pitching.

MIKE TORREZ: Mookie was kind of a quiet guy. He didn't say a lot. He was a great leadoff hitter for us, and could play the outfield as well as anybody. And hustled - he always hustled a lot. Mookie was always one of the instrumental players on our team.

CHARLIE PULEO: He was a great teammate. Always a smile on his face. He was always thrilled to be out there playing baseball. And a good centerfielder. You didn't mind him out there - he tracked balls down for you, and was an outstanding offensive player, also. He brought a lot of enthusiasm to the ballpark every night and it showed in the way he played.

~~Joel Youngblood~~

DAN NORMAN: He was a good player - he was with the Reds organization when I was there, then he got traded to the Mets [from the St. Louis Cardinals for Mike Phillips, on the same day as the "Midnight Massacre"]. And then, he was traded to the Expos when I was with the Expos. Good ballplayer, could play many positions. Played a long time. Good teammate.

PAT ZACHRY: Might have been the National League chess champion! Joel was a really wonderful outfielder. Could go get it, could throw it, could lay it out there on a string - just riffle it to third base as good as anybody, ever. Was a good hitter. Wasn't ever going to hit a lot for power, because he wasn't real big, but could play, could hit. He could run and throw and field as good as anybody. Joel signed in the winter of 1970, and I met him in the summer of 1970 - the year I signed. He was from Houston, and we drove home together a few times, and lived together a few times. Joel was one of my favorite teammates - he was a good guy.

CHAPTER 23:
SHEA & FANS

STEVE JACOBSON: It was an ugly building that the city built. The general manager was Johnny Murphy [from 1968-1969], and he read the criticism of what an industrial looking stadium it was. And he said, *"Do you want us to put a flower on it?"* And that's when...do you remember the metal squares that hung there, like a piece of non-representational art? That was a result of the press being so critical of what the building looked like!

GARY "BABA BOOEY" DELL'ABATE: I loved Shea Stadium. It's the first baseball place I'd ever been to. It transformed a lot over the years, but I remember the first time I went to Shea Stadium - like in the '60s - they had these weird corrugated orange and blue squares, attached to cables on the side. It was just so ugly! [The "squares" would be removed in 1980] People have said this over and over again, and I do agree with it - Shea Stadium was a dump, but it was *our* dump. And I did love that place. I'd gone to Yankee Stadium once, oddly for a non-Yankee game event - I think my dad was selling ice cream at the time, and he had to make a delivery, because Billy Graham's Crusade was there, and I remember going in and seeing Yankee Stadium that way.

I'd been there enough that I knew my way around Shea Stadium pretty well, and it was an interesting place. I remember even in like, '79 or '80, I had this really good friend that I worked at this dog supply store with, and he didn't seem like he was much of sports fan, but his best friend was a Pirates fan. So for like, three or four years in a row, his friend would buy Pirates/Mets tickets when the season started, and it was the best seats I ever sat in ever - even when I went with my dad - because he would buy them before the season started, and they were just easy to get good seats. We would be like, ten rows behind the Mets' dugout. I do remember going to a lot of Pirates games.

JERRY KOOSMAN: Shea Stadium was the park that I came up in, so it's kind of your "alma mater" - your home base. You saw a lot of things happen there. You left a lot of sweat on the mound. So you have some personal feelings and remembrances that seem to get torn down when the stadium leaves [Shea was demolished after the 2008 season]. There was just a lot of memories there and they'll always be there. Just because the stadium isn't there, you still have the memories.

CRAIG SWAN: I thought it was great. I got up there in '73, and it was kind of a state of the art stadium, still. Although there were many stadiums like Shea Stadium, there are not those many left, because everybody got a little more specialized. I think what I remember the most was how avid the fans were. Even the few thousand that we had there in the mid '70s, they were avid fans. That was the thing. I'm a Southern California boy, kind of a laidback, sailor/surfer type, and New Yorkers are *not* that way. [Laughs] It took me a while to adapt to that, but I grew to love it, because they had a passion for the game. In LA, they hardly boo - they read newspapers between pitches. It's not quite like the New York fans. So that's one thing that I remember about Shea, is the fans.

JOHN STEARNS: It was a culture shock for me. I lived in Manhattan for five years, I'm from Denver, Colorado. Shea Stadium was an older type of stadium, had grass, deep fences, it was a hard ballpark to hit in for power - unless you were Dave Kingman. I think the fans were great. They loved me a lot. For a few years there, I tried to go out and sign autographs before the game early - almost every day. Tried to give back what I was getting from all of them. I had a great time learning about New York, Manhattan, and the subway system, and not needing a car - you don't need a car in Manhattan. And I'd get out to Shea Stadium and all around.

GARY "BABA BOOEY" DELL'ABATE: I was probably about 15 or 16, and I remember my buddy and I would take the bus once or twice a summer, and then you'd get there and just buy a ticket. You didn't have to worry about getting to Shea Stadium and that the game was going to be sold out. We probably went to a couple of day games.

I remember the funny thing about those games was it would be packed with camp kids, and you could tell, because they would all be wearing the same shirts. You'd look to your left, and you'd see a sea of yellow shirts, and that was like, a YMCA camp. And I remember they were doing a lot of stuff like, selling group tickets to camps.

I remember my buddy and I, we got a huge discount by cutting a coupon on the side of a milk carton, because it would say, "Come see the Mets and get a ticket for $1.50" or something like that. But I also remember that we would buy the worst ticket in the house, we'd take our ticket, we'd go to where it was - which would almost be up top - and we'd go, "Well, why should we sit here? There seems to be a lot of available seats!"

CRAIG SWAN: That was noisy [the planes constantly flying over Shea during games]. I used to use that noise as much as I could - I was used to it because I played there. So if I heard a jet taking off at LaGuardia, I tried to time my pitch - my wind-up - right when it was the loudest part, so it would distract the hitter. I tried to pitch during those flyovers. A pitcher will use anything he can!

DAN NORMAN: I remember the planes going over all the time. Sometimes you couldn't hear the cutoff man because of the planes jetting over!

PAT ZACHRY: *Loud.* Every three minutes, a jet flying over. Sure was nice on a Sunday afternoon or even a Saturday afternoon, but for the most part, it was just loud. And a memorable place. There will never be another one like Shea.

CHARLIE PULEO: To me, it was the most exciting thing I ever did. I grew up idolizing the Mets, and getting the opportunity to play at Shea, with everything that went on there in 1969, to me, it was a thrill every time I walked on the field and walked in the clubhouse - to know I'm in the same place that some of those guys that played and I grew up idolizing. I pitched in Yankee Stadium, I pitched in Detroit, and there was nothing like putting on the Mets uniform and being out there in New York as a member of the Mets. It was a thrill every time, and a good ballpark to pitch in. At that time, it was 390 in the power alleys and 410 in centerfield. I think Bill Madlock almost killed Mookie Wilson one night - he hit a ball off the centerfield [wall], and I think he knocked him right into the centerfield wall! But it was a great place to pitch.

RICK OWNBEY: Pitching in Shea Stadium I absolutely loved. High mound, natural grass, tremendous fans. They were very, very good to me.

BRENT GAFF: All those stadiums, you're just awestruck standing out in the middle of that, looking up. I remember in my debut, standing on the mound, and looking straight up at the sky…and there's people up there! I never played in a venue like that before. You never get tired of being on a major league field - that's for sure. It's a thrill, no matter what's going on, that you can even step out there. I felt very lucky to have an opportunity like that.

TOM GORMAN: You had to walk through the bowels of Shea to get to the dugout, and there would be rats running around and stuff like that! You'd walk down a plank. When I first walked down there, I thought, *"This is Shea Stadium?"* Because you're literally underneath the seats, and it's scary under there. But when you got out there, other than the planes, it was a great place to pitch. It always seemed like the wind was blowing in. Sometimes, you'd pitch in Chicago, and you feel like you can touch left field, because the wind is howling out to left. We always seemed to have a little bit of a wind coming in, so that was good.

PAT ZACHRY: I've never been out to the new one [Citi Field, which opened in 2009], so I couldn't tell you what the comparison would be completely. But anytime you're in a big league stadium, it's a good place. Even the old San Francisco ballpark [Candlestick Park]. As long as it was big leagues, you were doing good.

JOHN STEARNS: The Jets shared the stadium [from 1964-1983]. I just remember they had their locker room open when we were playing in August and September. But I didn't have too much contact with them. You realized that they were there, and we ran into them once in a while, but we didn't see too much of them. When we were playing at home, they were out of there. You could see where they had the lines in the field and everything, but they tried to make it get back to baseball as close as possible. And they did a pretty good job on that. It's always fun to be able to meet other athletes from another sport.

DAN NORMAN: The main thing I remember about Shea Stadium is that guy holding up the signs all the time. [Laughs] If you did something on the field that he didn't care for, he'd put up a big old sign, and you know the TV cameras would catch it. I have no idea who the guy was [Karl Ehrhardt], but he was a popular figure there at Shea Stadium. He'd put a sign up, and it made me laugh - unless it was about me!

JERRY KOOSMAN: There was so much through the years - banner day and bat day and hat day, and the artist with the signs, and the organ player. Just putting it all together put vibrations in the air, that create memories, also. They helped create the excitement, and they would get us excited. And when you've got fans that interested and knowledgeable, you want to play a little harder. There's nothing you're going to get by in front of those fans, because they know the sport better than anybody in the US.

BOBBY VALENTINE: We tried to do a lot of promotions. We did camera days and banner days - we did anything to get people in the ballpark. They did the bubblegum blowing contest - I think that was a national thing put on by Topps. I was always blowing bubbles in the dugout and chewing gum, so that was pretty easy for me. I think actually, the measuring stick broke the bubble - it was getting bigger at the time [Valentine beat out Ed Kranepool for "biggest bubble" in the 1978 contest].

JOHN STEARNS: Banner Day was the day that everybody came in and walked around the infield with their signs, and their long banners stretched out. We were all out there too - the players. I had a lot of fun on Banner Day.

CRAIG SWAN: Opening day, we'd usually have 50,000. By next day, we'd have 3,000. I kind of liked it, because I somehow connected with the fans, so I was always having a good time with them. And when you only had 2,000 or 3,000, the ushers would eventually let them down by the field, and you got to know them. And of course, I had my garden out in the bullpen. After Joe Pignatano - our bullpen coach - taught me to garden, then I built it into just this *huge* garden. You could walk down there as a fan, and you would be on the second level, but you could see well into the bullpen. I would give fans a tour of the garden! Like, "Here's the tomatoes, and here's the green beans." I had fun with them.

JERRY KOOSMAN: Well, you can't blame the fans. If you're not winning and you're not putting exciting teams out there, why come and watch?

JOHN STEARNS: I never heard the name "Grant's Tomb," but I did know we were only drawing 10,000 a game - sometimes less.

STEVE JACOBSON: DiamondVision [which debuted at Shea in 1982] was a product of Jim Nagourney - he was the vice president in charge of things like that. And I liked Nagourney. I live in Long Beach, and he had been a city manager of Long Beach some years before that. And he and his wife were having dinner at my home, and my son was back from college, and he noted the paintjob that they had put on Shea Stadium. And he said, *"Who put that awful paint on Shea Stadium?"* And it was Nagourney, across the table! It was a purplish blue, and it was unsightly.

GARY "BABA BOOEY" DELL'ABATE: I thought that Big Apple thing [which debuted at Shea in 1981] was cheesy since the day that they installed it, but I still liked it. And it was something to be excited about. The DiamondVision, I think the Mets had installed it, like probably one of the last people in baseball to put it in - as they usually are with everything! It's sort of like by the time they got it, it wasn't that exciting, because everybody else had one.

JOHN STEARNS: When the apple went up? That was exciting. The old Shea Stadium, that kind of takes you back to a different era. They were building stadiums in the '60s and '70s that weren't quite…I guess it was a step up from the stadiums they built in the '20s and '30s, but Shea Stadium wasn't too much of a stadium, like they build them now. I think Camden Yards was the first one that was more "modern," should I say. Shea Stadium was kind of just a cement block with seats in it. But those two things you mentioned, they were fun. DiamondVision was a precursor to today's updated scoreboards. It was a step in the right direction. It was cool, for those days.

TIM McCARVER: Mets fans were fabulous. They always rooted for the underdog in New York City. And obviously, since their beginning, innately, in 1962, when they lost 120 games, they became "The Lovable Losers." And then seven years later, they became lovable winners - "The Miracle of '69." But I still find under the surface, Mets fans, their fervor is nonpareil. Because they're really for the underdog in New York City, and everybody says that New York City, with the Yankees and their reputation, and 27 World Series winners and 40 pennants - they are such direct opposites of the Yankees. I mean, the Yankees are arguably the greatest name in the history of sports in the world. Maybe Manchester United could top that - maybe some soccer teams. But the Yankee logo is very strong. And I always found it interesting and warm that lovable losers like the Mets turned into lovable winners, and the toast of the town in the '80s.

LENNY RANDLE: The Met fans were phenomenal. They had signs, they had kids wearing look-alike clothes - we thought some of the kids were us in the stands! It was amazing to see the "artistic chanting" - it was almost like a choir on certain days. It was like, Boyz II Men and the Backstreet Boys in that section, and then it would be New

Kids on the Block over in this section - it was like they rehearsed. It was amazing to watch that rehearsal. Now see, in Arizona State, we were used to crowds of 10,000-15,000 people. And I guess Shea was maybe 20,000-30,000 when we came there. It seemed like they were an organized choir.

They were energetic, entertaining, funny, comical...I mean, Pete Rose used to love sliding into third, just to talk to the guy at third sitting in the seats. I think most guys loved playing at Shea - it just turned them on. I saw Garvey, Lasorda, Reggie Smith, Dusty, Buckner, and guys change at Shea - they're a whole different person. Shea fans motivated the other team, or the guy would go south. It would either pump a guy up or he'd go, "This is my day off, because they're all over me." They'd either take the ridicule, or they were mediocre that day, like, *"Let me get out of here!"*

STEVE JACOBSON: They were pretty good fans. They came out and they understood what was going on there. I think the New York fans - baseball fans - were very hip. And they knew when players tried hard. I remember when Tino Martinez left the Yankees, he said he liked playing here, because the fans realized how hard you tried.

PAT ZACHRY: *Loud.* When they showed up there, like on a Sunday afternoon game or Saturday afternoon game...loud. And they loved to support the home team. That was an important thing - we knew that when certain teams came to town, we could always count on a few extra fans coming out. They were going to razz Pete and Johnny and that bunch, and razz Schmidt and Luzinski and those guys, and anybody else. They were strictly behind their Met players at the time - that was always good to know.

JOHN STEARNS: I always tried to sign as much as possible. I'd go out and sign in the stadium before the games. I still get a lot of fan mail - people find you. I get two or three letters almost every day in the mail, with "Please sign my old cards and send them back." I send them all right back - it's the least that I can do, that a major league player can do is to return a request of an autograph to somebody. It could be the other way around - you could not be getting *any* letters or autographs, and that means that nobody gives a damn about you. So I feel like it's an obligation almost - to give back to the fans what they've given back to you, the opportunity to be a big league baseball player and star.

DAN NORMAN: Mets fans are loyal. And they want to win every year. You can't win every year, but they want you to win. They would show up every game, whether there was rain there or the sun shining.

RANDY JONES: I thought the Mets fans were great. They were opinionated, and they let you know when you were good and they let you know when you were bad. And I bought into that. I didn't have any problem with that at all. I liked their passion and I had fun with them. I'd go back and go to get in my truck when we were done with a game, and if I hadn't pitched well, they'd be all over me - "Randy, you didn't pitch well." And I'd say, *"I know, man.* I'm having trouble. Struggling." I'd just talk to them - I had no problem at all with it, and pitching there. At the end of '82, I got real comfortable there at Shea, finally. In '81, I don't know if I ever did. '82 I really did - I started feeling pretty comfortable on the mound and getting used to everything, and everything fits in your eye a little bit better. But unfortunately, I hurt my arm too soon that season.

TOM GORMAN: I had no problem with the Mets fans. Doug [Sisk] had a little bit of a problem there, when he was getting booed at home - we didn't take too lightly to that. Doug did have some issues with balls and strikes, and then the fans get on you. But the fans treated me really well - I never had a problem with them.

BRENT GAFF: They were good. That was one good thing - they put up with me. I never got booed or nothing. They probably should have! In the paper - I think it was the Daily News or somebody - at the All-Star Break, they would send out a report card, and in '84 I got a "B+" which I was pretty proud of. I don't now who votes on that - probably the writers - but the fans were always nice.

New Yorkers are different. I've never played at Yankee Stadium, but yeah, New Yorkers…they're not the nicest people around compared to the rest of the country, I don't think. I didn't like New York - it was the last place I wanted to play. I'm an old hick from hillbilly town, y'know? It was overwhelming to me - I didn't want to go downtown, I didn't want to go to Manhattan. Nobody was friendly, you couldn't even smile at anybody or say "Hi" without somebody thinking you're going to rob them or whatever. And playing in Mississippi and Virginia and all the different places I played, everybody's always nice. New York…it's a tough town.

PETE FALCONE: To go through those years with us, and to show up like that, and to be as energetic as they were, you've got to tip your hat to the Mets fans back then. There was very little to cheer about. [Laughs]

STEVE ZABRISKIE: I know people who root for both the Mets and the Yankees, because they love *New York baseball* - it's not a mutually exclusive thing. My favorite one of those fans is Billy Crystal. Billy is a New York baseball fan, and he will tell you that. And I think there are many of them like that. The fans were behind this team when Casey was there and they stunk. When the Mets became good and were winning, it was off the charts. Unbelievable.

GARY "BABA BOOEY" DELL'ABATE: I was definitely a Mets/Jets/Islanders fan as a kid, because if you grew up on Long Island, from my house to Shea Stadium was probably 40 minutes. From my house to Yankee Stadium was probably an hour and 20 minutes - with traffic. And if you loved the Jets, the Mets and Jets shared the same house, so it just was a natural progression. Whereas the Yankees and the Giants shared the same place for a long time. Back then, there definitely is a whole "Long Island connection" to the Mets - there's no doubt.

But back then, there was a time where you chose a team for *a reason.* Again, I chose the team because it was my dad's team. But the notion now, that I can never get behind - "Oh, I'm a really big Oakland A's fan because I love the yellow and the green" is the most ridiculous thing I have ever heard! Back then, you chose a team because you liked a team, because you knew the players - not because the jersey looked good on you. For me, again, I grew up in a house that was a "National League house." So I was a National League fan. I didn't even know what was going on with the Cleveland Indians or the Detroit Tigers, but I sure as hell knew what was going on with the Reds and the Pirates. They just seemed like "the big bad Yankees," and I guess you chose sides early. And once you chose sides, you're stuck with them.

CHAPTER 24:
ANNOUNCERS & MEDIA

GARY "BABA BOOEY" DELL'ABATE: I loved all those Mets broadcasters, and I still love it when I see the old broadcasts today. They were so great, because they were so..."broadcaster-y." [Laughs] Bob Murphy had such a broadcaster voice, and Lindsey Nelson was legendary for his ugly jacket - my dad would always get a kick out of that. The Mets for me was a huge bonding thing with my dad - we would always watch the games together, we would goof on Lindsey Nelson's jackets.

And the thing that I remember about Kiner is I was always asking my dad, "Who is Ralph Kiner?" And my father used to refer him as "the best worst guy in the Hall of Fame." My dad would say, "He was basically a home run hitter - that was all he ever did - but he hit so many home runs in such a short period of time [in a career that spanned ten seasons from 1946-1955, Kiner hit 369 homers]. And he used to date starlets." And I would look at this old guy, and go, *"Really?"* He just looked like an old dude to me - especially as a kid.

But we would always watch 'Kiner's Korner,' which was just a mainstay. You had to watch the Mets game, and then you had to follow it with 'Kiner's Korner,' because it was just such a riot. And he would always give out some really terrible gift. "Here's a $20 gift certificate to Timex Watch" or something like that - some bad steakhouse. But we loved him.

My greatest memory of Kiner is it would be the middle of the season, and it would be really slow, he would tell this story that went on for like two innings, and would tell it over and over and over again. The core of the story was that he had led the league in home runs when he was playing for the Pirates, but they had come in last, and Branch Rickey was the general manager of the Pirates at that point. And he went to Branch Rickey, and he said, "I want a raise." And Branch Rickey said to him, "How many home runs did you hit last year?" And he said, "39." "What place did we come in last year?" "Last." And Branch Rickey said, "You know what? *I can come in last without you.*" But he would tell that story every year. It would get to the point where I would go, "He's going to tell that story again!"

But they were all great characters. I don't remember Bob Murphy ever laughing. He was just a very serious but really good play-by-play guy. And Kiner would chime in with those goofy stories. I don't even know how they put that team together. Like, why would the Mets want to have an ex-Pirate as their announcer? I guess they had nobody - there was no history of the Mets before that, so that's how they got him.

STEVE JACOBSON: Kiner, everybody who was around, loved Ralph. He was a really good storyteller, and would talk himself into a corner - y'know, create a sentence from which there was no exit - but he was very good. And could be a decent critic. He wasn't entirely a homer, like a lot of broadcasters are. Ralph could be critical - not painfully critical - but he could make a comment about a player, that a player wouldn't like to hear. And he was a fascinating storyteller - going back to World War II [Kiner served as a US Navy pilot] and later playing with the Pittsburgh Pirates, which were as bad a team as there was, until the first Mets came along.

Murphy was a professional journeyman. I don't think that he had nearly the impact on me, but he was a nice fellow, and he was a pretty good broadcaster. He wasn't Vin Scully and he wasn't as interesting as Ralph Kiner, but he was pretty frank. I remember a 15-inning game, and his comment when it was over was, *"They finally win the damn thing!"* I shouldn't put Murphy down - I don't intend to - but he was not somebody that you would vote for the Hall of Fame.

PAT ZACHRY: Those were the sweetest old guys [Kiner and Murphy]. They tried - they really, really tried - to keep us "built up" on the air, to keep it interesting. Just tremendous gentlemen. Such nice people. Bob Murphy went out of his way to try and help us, and Kiner always did as much as he could, trying to make everything look a lot better than it really was. And of course, there was always his show, 'Kiner's Korner.'

TOM GORMAN: I did [appear on 'Kiner's Korner']. A game that I threw seven innings against Pittsburgh in my start, I got to go on Ralph's show - it was actually me and Bobby Bailor, the shortstop, went on together. That was kind of exciting. And Tim McCarver, he was great, and Murph was awesome. We all traveled together, so they were part of the team - along with 25 reporters, too. It's just like anything - when you're living with somebody pretty much for seven or eight months out of the year, you're going to run into some problems. That was probably, looking back, how many teams have 20 reporters traveling with them, on the plane and such? That was kind of a touchy deal - to keep them at bay. But when you looked at it, they knew that if they reported whatever that was on the plane, that they wouldn't be on the plane next time. No, I never had a problem with them. I remember Ralph calling Gary Carter "Gary Cooper," which I thought was hilarious...but that could have been after a few! [Laughs]

STEVE ZABRISKIE: Bob was one of the greatest guys you will ever meet. He was so dedicated to the Mets and to his craft as an announcer. Murph loved radio, radio loved Murph - he had the perfect voice. He knew the game, he loved the game. I'm sure you're one of them that has so many memories of Murph's voice on the radio calling the game. It was classic baseball on the radio. Murph was so dedicated. You just always knew that sadly, in the future sometime, Murph is going to die in the booth. Like a solider that dies with his boots on. Because that was his life. That was who he was. That was everything to him.

He didn't really care I don't think about developing a persona outside of who he was, because who he was was who you heard on the radio. Murph was Murph. And he loved the Mets, and he bled orange and blue. He lived and died with that team. That came across on the air, and fans responded to that. There was anguish in his voice, there was so much excitement in his voice. And radio was the perfect medium for that, because you paint the picture on radio. And Murph was so good at sharing his emotion and painting the picture with the audience - with the fans. And a fun guy to be around.

CRAIG SWAN: One of the things I'd like to say about Murph is through all those terrible years the Mets had in the late '70s and early '80s, you couldn't tell that if you listened to Murph on the radio, because it sounded like he had so much enthusiasm - it was just nice to be around him. And I got to know him pretty well. And Ralph too, was just a sweet, sweet man. Going on 'Kiner's Korner' was kind of fun. Although he got the names wrong half the time, we didn't care. I don't know if you knew that about Ralph - he called Milner "Matlack," and he'd get the names mixed up all the time. [Laughs] I loved both of them. I even got to be around Lindsey Nelson early on, with all the strange sports coats he'd wear every day!

JERRY KOOSMAN: Yeah, probably a couple hundred times [Koosman appeared on 'Kiner's Korner']! Ralph Kiner, Bob Murphy, and Lindsey Nelson - three great announcers that were just perfect for each other. They got along well, they were fun to be with. They flew with us all the time, they were part of the family, and you got to know each other's families and each other personally really well. It was a treat having those guys announce the games. And if you were in the clubhouse or wherever you were, you listened to them. Lindsey Nelson, my wife sometimes wished he wouldn't announce, because she said he made the games *too* exciting - she'd get too nervous when I was pitching! [Laughs]

JOHN STEARNS: Yeah, I was on 'Kiner's Korner' several times. Bob Murphy was a great guy - I used to listen to him when I wasn't playing. When I came up as a rookie, they were already there, they helped me blend in as a teammate, talked to me a lot - I was on a lot of interviews with them. And I became the #1 catcher, and then all of a sudden, I was going to the All-Star Game a lot, so they liked me. I was one of the better players in those years when we were down on the team, and I got a lot of opportunities to be interviewed by those guys. It was just a lot of fun. They knew what they were doing. I enjoyed getting interviewed and didn't feel intimidated by it at all. I thought that it was a really fun time to be with those two guys. And then knowing that Ralph Kiner...I started looking at his stats - God, he was a tremendous home run hitter. And it was just fun hanging out with those guys.

CHARLIE PULEO: That was another big thrill for me - to meet Bob Murphy and Ralph Kiner. I met Lindsey Nelson later on here in Tennessee, at a banquet. I grew up listening to them on the TV and radio. And to actually meet Bob Murphy and Ralph Kiner personally is unbelievable. And then to get on 'Kiner's Korner'...the only problem with 'Kiner's Korner' was he would get me and Orosco and some of these guys confused once in a while. He'd call us by different names!

I was on there one time, and he said, "Charlie, you struggled with your control tonight." And I said, "Ralph, *I only walked one guy."* It was always great to be on the show, but you always knew something was going to come up. I was on with Mookie Wilson one time, and he called him Hubie Brooks! Bob Murphy was always very kind. I enjoyed talking to him. They were great. I wish Lindsey Nelson would have still been with them at that time, also [Nelson's last year as a Mets broadcaster was 1978]. But getting to meet Lindsey later on was also a big thrill.

WALT TERRELL: I sure did [go on 'Kiner's Korner']. It was a thrill. A good man, thoroughly enjoyed that...I'm trying to think if Tim McCarver just started there. Obviously, Bob Murphy was there, Steve Zabriskie had started there, and there was a guy that was on with Bob Murphy...I'm looking right at him, I cant think of his name [Terrell later recalled it was Steve LaMar]. But those guys were more "TV guys," for WOR at the time - Zabriskie and McCarver. But they were great to me. Everybody was good. Hell, they treated me better than I probably deserved, how's that? The writers, radio people, TV people treated me wonderful. Good deal. They were all good folks.

TIM McCARVER: In 1977, I had had a good year [with the Philadelphia Phillies], and there's nothing better for a player for people to say that he's finished, and then he resurfaces for that last hurrah. And my last hurrah came about because I had run into a left-hander with a good move to first base, and that was Steve Carlton. So I had a good year that year, and Toronto was coming into being, and Toronto asked for permission to speak with me - even though I was still playing for the Phillies. And we had won the division in 1976, and I remember I was asking for $80,000, and Toronto was offering me $30,000 for a four-year deal [as a broadcaster], and I was going to work with Tom Cheek. And the Phillies got wind of that, and Bill Giles said, "Well give you want you want in 1977, and then we'll give you a two-year contract whenever your playing career is up, and you can be an announcer." I had been with the Phillies before, so they knew me - even though I didn't have any broadcasting experience.

So I had a better year in 1977, and I led the team in hitting, even though it was half as many at-bats as the regulars. But then I signed a two-year deal in '78 and '79 - keep in mind, I had that two-year deal with the Phillies, so I retired in '79 as an active player, and started broadcasting in 1980. In 1981, I was kind of the fifth guy in a four-man broadcasting booth. And I got a lot of experience from Harry Kalas, Andy Musser, Richie Ashburn, and Chris Wheller. But I was certainly not in a spot where I was going to take over any of their jobs. So the Mets asked me if I'd be interested in coming to New York, and I had just gotten settled with my family and my wife at the time, and I said, "No." So I came back in 1982 to be a broadcaster for the Phillies, and the Mets called again at the end of the season - so they called me twice in the 1982 season. And I was dabbling with ABC at the time and working with Dick Enberg, and Bob Costas and I in 1980 did our first network broadcast together. Well, it was even *more evident* that I was the fifth broadcaster in a four-man crew.

STEVE ZABRISKIE: I was working for ABC Sports. I was doing Major League Baseball and College Football, which I did or ABC for over 20 years. I really was interested in being with a team, because I had had a taste of it - in '78, I did the Angels games on television, with Don Drysdale, whenever Dick Enberg would be gone, to do football or something else. Dick Enberg was the play-by-play guy. So I filled in for Dick, and kind of found out what it was like to follow a team, be with a team on a local or regional broadcast. There was a lot of turmoil going on at ABC at the time, so my agent started putting feelers out there, if any major league teams were looking for announcers. And it actually came down to the Houston Astros and the Mets.

I was a little bit torn, because I had gone to the University of Houston, and had some connections there. But the prospects of working with a team in New York would be exciting - even though the Mets at the time were horrible. I was trying to decide, and I got a call from Al Harazin on Christmas Eve in 1982, and he said, "I just want you to know we just signed Tim McCarver to be one of our TV announcers." Well, Timmy and I had known each other for some time. In fact, when Timmy quit playing in 1980, I actually auditioned him for ABC. He and I did a baseball game together as an audition for him, as a color guy. And we really hit it off. So when Al called me and told me that they had signed Timmy, that sort of made my decision for me right there, because I was on the fence a little bit, still. And I was immediately excited to go join the Mets, which I did, and never regretted it, because I had some really good years and a lot of fun.

TIM McCARVER: I commuted some of the time. I still had my home in Philadelphia, and I was living in the city. I spent a lot of time at the ballpark. Very few people beat me to the ballpark. [Laughs] And that remains the case today. I'm with the Cardinals now, and I'm working with Dan McLaughlin, and I told him, many, many times last year, he's the only broadcaster who ever beat me to the ballpark. And I take pride in that. I mean, you have to totally immerse yourself in the business. So I'd get there at 3:00/3:30 in the afternoon. I put in a lot of time at the ballpark - but you've got to do that.

STEVE ZABRISKIE: I did the games that were on WOR. Once in a while, I would fill in with SportsChannel, on the Cable side. And a couple of times, due to either illness or some other conflict, a couple of games on radio - I think only twice did I actually do a radio game, when we were not televising, to fill in for Murph or somebody. I don't really remember. But basically my whole stint was WOR.

Rusty Staub [who later joined the broadcast team in 1986] is just one of the greatest guys of all-time. Rusty and I became very close. Rusty was a unique person - he's a man of many talents, and he has some quirkiness to him. And when he was a player, he had certain little - as all players do - rituals or superstitions or things about what they have to do every day. And he's particular about certain things. And that is something that maybe bothers some people, but I always found it to be very endearing, because I'm probably unoffendable, thankfully. But Rusty is just golden, as far as I'm concerned.

I felt that Rusty brought a really refreshing and interesting view to the game. He was obviously not trained as a broadcaster, and he had a lot to learn in the beginning, but I had hoped that he would stay around longer - I don't really know the particulars of why he didn't, during that period [Rusty remained a Mets broadcaster through 1995]. But I thoroughly enjoyed any opportunity I got to work with Rusty. He inducted me into a special brotherhood that he's had for years, or a lot of friends of his in New York, and it was an honor. We would have meetings at this restaurant periodically, and because I lived in Orlando at the time, he made me the special ambassador to Florida! Which is a made up title, but it was a lot of fun. It just so happened that when the Mets clinched in '86 [on September 17th, against the Chicago Cubs], Rusty and I happened to be on the air together. So that was kind of special.

TIM McCARVER: My career as a New York Met broadcaster opened me up to the networks in New York. I went to the networks while still doing the Mets, and broadcasted through 1998 with New York.

STEVE ZABRISKIE: I couldn't have been more blessed to have those guys [McCarver and Kiner] as partners.

RANDY JONES: The PR guy is the same guy for the Mets still, today - Jay Horwitz [who joined the Mets in 1980]. When the Mets come into town [San Diego], I make sure I swing by, find Jay, and say hello to him. Because he was there when I played for the Mets. I go, "It's amazing Jay. You've been tricking them this many years? *My God!"*

STEVE JACOBSON: I became a columnist [covering the Mets for Newsday] in '79. So I wasn't with them all the time, as I had split between the Mets and the Yankees for about 20 years before that. The press box is the press box [at Shea Stadium]. The issue that made one team better to cover than the other was not so much the physical problems - although the elevator at Shea Stadium was a little bit easier - but it was the excitement of being at the game, and working the game when something good or something interesting or new might happen. And it wasn't happening with the Mets [during the late '70s/early '80s]. It wasn't the first choice to cover on any day - except when the visiting team was in town, and you wound up writing often about the other team.

JOHN STEARNS: I thought [the New York press] was fine. I didn't have any problem with the press at all. [Daily News writer] Jack Lang was a good guy - he was trying to do his job. Marty Noble was there a lot, and Dick Young. I didn't have a problem with any of the writers, really. I thought they were fun. They've got to do a job and you try to get in there and help them as much as you can. I never really had a run-in - I don't think - with a writer.

BRENT GAFF: I didn't like them. I didn't know. Nowadays, they kind of give you a clue, because coming up in the minor leagues…in Triple A, there's just one [reporter] you'd have to talk to. You could get to know him a little bit. But in New York, I probably said some shit I never should have. But nobody ever told me. I think now, they have meetings and they teach these young kids, "OK, here's what you say to the media. Don't be sticking your foot in your mouth or making us look stupid, or saying dumb shit." And nobody told me, so I probably didn't do it right. But they were tough. I didn't have nothing nice to say about going from the White House to the Shit House in less than a month. I'm thinking they helped get me sent down faster than anything. But you guys have got to tell it like it is.

From what I heard and what I experienced, it's probably the toughest place you can play would be New York, because of the media. If you're not that sharp talking to people like that, I think that comes with age - if you're in the big leagues four or five years, you probably learn all that shit. But as a rookie, you're out there kind of blindfolded, like, "I don't know what's going on. What should I say?" I'm thinking they should have told me there was going to be that kind of pressure on me right off the bat. Like, "Look dummy, don't say *this.*"

Because my major league debut, right before I'm starting, there's like a dozen guys asking me questions, and I'm trying to get my shit together to go out and pitch, and when I got called up, I had like two days before I started. I said, "Davey, who's in town, anyway?" He said, "Well, they're playing the Dodgers right now." They were the world champs the year before, and I'm going over all these players in my head, and talking to everybody about, "How would you pitch Cey or so-and-so?" I get there, and we're playing the Giants, and they're asking me about the Giants before the game, and I said, "Shit, I really wanted to throw against the Dodgers. My major league debut, and I'm getting to pitch against the world champs in my debut - that's who I thought I was going to pitch against."

Well one of the reporters runs over and tells the Giants, "This punk don't even give a shit about you guys. He wanted to throw against the Dodgers. Evidently, he don't think you're good enough" or whatever. So it was a big stink about that, and that ain't what I meant. Like I said, just another dumb move that I made, that I never even thought about. I was just prepared to throw against the Dodgers. But they spun it into, "Let's tell them what he said. Let's see if we can get some shit started." And it did. It was in the paper. The San Francisco paper - "GAFF POPS OFF, OVERLOOKS OUR TEAM, GETS BEAT" or whatever.

RANDY JONES: The press in the old days was in on everybody's ass, if you weren't playing good. And they were fair - they praised you when you did good, and they got on you when you didn't. I never could argue with the press and the media in New York.

CHAPTER 25:
METS & YANKS

GARY "BABA BOOEY" DELL'ABATE: I do remember the Yankees won the two world championships [in 1977 and 1978], and listen, it is always, always, always going to be tough being a Mets fan in the city - no matter what. I remember Todd Zeile [who played for the Mets from 2000-2001, and again in 2004], he had just gotten traded to the Mets, and I ran into him at an event and we chatted. I said, "I warn you right now, just so you know - *you'll always be a second class citizen in this town.* Even when you go to a World Series. Because even if you win the World Series two years in a row, you're still 25 shy of the Yankees, and they'll always rub that in your face." So that's what it was like. It was like, the Mets are bad, and the Yankees were good, so you always had to deal with that. But the whole point of being a fan is going through the lean years is what makes the great years worth it.

PETE FALCONE: The Yankees were the Yankees - look at the teams they had. I think we beat them a few times in spring training, if I recall. But they were a lot better team than we were. And they got the attention because they deserved it. They had an "All-Star team" out there.

WALT TERRELL: Honestly, when you're playing, you're worried more about yourself than what's going on in other places. And not that you don't read or hear about or see those things, but you've got your own deal to take care of. Hell, I want to stay in the big leagues and want to get to the big leagues - if the Yankees are ten games in front, that doesn't affect me none whatsoever. Just for me, no, it wasn't a distraction or anything else. I didn't really give a damn.

STEVE HENDERSON: My main focus was on the Mets. I never thought about over there in the American League. I didn't think about that too much.

LENNY RANDLE: No, we didn't look at it like that, because we didn't see a better team - we just saw more fans than Shea. And Billy Martin - who I had as a manager in Texas - automatically draws a million people, by himself. So we knew that 15,000 or 30,000 people would come to see or heckle Billy Martin - who should be in the Hall of Fame, by the way. And he was that kind of charismatic manager - being a former Yankee and bringing all the guys back. Even the guys from Joe DiMaggio and Yogi, saying, "I'm never going back, because I didn't get eight tickets or I didn't get a ball" or whatever reasons. Because we heard all the stories.

And when Billy came back, all that resentment and hate for management for their era, they forgot it all. So the Yankees fan base went up. All of our fan base would have come back if we had Rusty Staub, Tommie Agee, and Nolan Ryan and all those guys come back - we would have had probably an equal fan base and an equal gate, having events with former players. So I didn't look at Roy White being better than Steve Henderson, or Elliott Maddox being better than Mickey Rivers, because we all felt equal - it's just pinning it on game style and pitching.

CHARLIE PULEO: Well, my roommate from college at Seton Hall was [Yankees catcher] Rick Cerone. So Rick was over with New York at the time, and we had a lot of fun with that for a while. I remember one night, we were both on the news. I wasn't jealous - growing up being a Mets fan, I didn't even think about the Yankees. They had Horace Clarke and all those guys back then - no disrespect to any of those guys, but they weren't very good at that time, and the Mets were really doing well when I was a kid. I didn't think about the Yankees. I was thrilled to be a New York Met - except for the fact that my roommate was over there. We had some fun with that. Other than that, I was a New York Met, and that was enough.

CRAIG SWAN: It was a different league - we didn't play each other back then, except the Mayor's Trophy Game. I knew the Met fans were into it, or the New York fans. But it wasn't something that I was concerned about. As long as you're in the big leagues, I figured I was doing pretty good.

STEVE JACOBSON: [The Mayor's Trophy Game] was - in the early years - great fun. And marvelous plays by Choo-Choo Coleman, to throw out a runner at second base who had never left first. Things like that. But the scheduling became so difficult, that they couldn't get the two teams together on an off day, and there were so few off days.

GARY "BABA BOOEY" DELL'ABATE: I never went to one, but we used to talk about it all the time. It was always goofy, because it was totally meaningless, but as kids, we thought it was the most important game ever. And my father would always chuckle and go, "They're not even trying. It doesn't even mean anything." But to us, it seemed like such a big deal - "Oh, the Yankees won the World Series, but we beat them, which means we could win." In memory, it was just a dumb game.

JOHN STEARNS: I have one memory and I'll tell you about this. We were a bad team and the Yankees were winning, so we're playing the game one day, and it's like '77. I've been in the big leagues maybe two years. I'm not really established yet, but I'm having a good year. The first part of the year, I had a really good year, and then the last part of '77 I faded a little bit. But we had the Mayor's

Trophy Game at Shea Stadium. We're taking batting practice, and the Yankees come out and start to get loose. And Reggie Jackson comes up behind the batting cage there, and he starts popping off, and he says, "The New York Mets...*the worst team in baseball.*" He's just really a jerk - so everybody could hear.

And I was standing right there, and I came *this close* to just decking him with a right hand shot to the cheek. Because he deserved that - he was being arrogant and loud, and was demeaning us. Had I had been like, one year older and one more year experienced, I would have dropped him right there. There's no doubt about it. I didn't do that, but I always remember that - Reggie Jackson coming up and taunting us, to our faces, in the Mayor's Trophy Game, during batting practice. I'm glad I didn't [punch Jackson], because it would have been a big fracas, if I had hit him. I've always thought about that - I'm sure I would have been fined and called down to the commissioner's office, and I would have just told the commissioner's office the truth, that Reggie Jackson came up behind our batting cage and was just demeaning us, egregiously.

PETE FALCONE: I only recall one Mayor's Trophy Game, and that was at Yankee Stadium. I think it was 1982. I think Rusty Staub hit a home run or something. But we won one game there, and it was great to be in Yankee Stadium and play there. I never played at Yankee Stadium other than that one time - other than our high school championship, we played at Yankee Stadium.

CHARLIE PULEO: Yes I did [play in the 1982 Mayor's Trophy Game]. It was over at Yankee Stadium. That's where I pitched, and I faced all of them. I pitched about five innings, I believe. Cerone was hurt. He had a broken hand or something, and he didn't play in that Mayor's Trophy Game. But it was fun. The thing I remember about it is when I went to the visiting clubhouse to get dressed, the Red Sox were in town the night before. They still had the tape up on the lockers of the names of the guys that were on the Red Sox. So I went into Carl Yastrzemski's locker. I thought that was neat - I dressed in his locker for that Mayor's Trophy Game.

RICK OWNBEY: The other game that really stuck out for me in '83 was I happened to have started the interleague game against the Yankees - at home. That was exciting. I believe I went three or four innings, and you're talking about Randolph, Nettles, and Winfield. The Mets fans were all cheering because I was one of the "new and upcoming stars." It was like 3-2 [against Winfield], and I just kept throwing high gas, and he kept swinging and fouling them off - but I think I finally struck him out. Just to hear the Mets fans go nuts was a great feeling.

CHARLIE PULEO: I believe it was a benefit for the Boys and Girls Clubs in New York City or the Little Leagues in the City. So it was a great thing to raise some money. Now, with the advent of the interleague play and the Yankees and the Mets playing that six game series, it took a lot of it away. But it was a great game at that time. And it drew good crowds and a lot of attention.

CRAIG SWAN: They were meaningless, so you'd have your starters out there for maybe two innings, and then put the other guys in. The other thing I remember is it used to take up one of our off days, and we didn't get many off days during the season, and here's a meaningless game we have to play. On an off day, I'd rather be with my family. So I didn't like them. I didn't like the exhibition games we played at West Point, although it was nice to go up there and play those. They were meaningless games, and again, we didn't get many days off. That was a long season. And a lot of our days off, we traveled, so it wasn't like a day off.

So I didn't like the exhibition. I thought 162 games were enough. But I know the fans liked them.

JOHN STEARNS: From a baseball standpoint, it was fun playing in Yankee Stadium. The House That Ruth Built and everything. It was a privilege to go to a place like that, and play a baseball game there, and be in the big leagues.

LENNY RANDLE: That Yankee team [that Randle played for in 1979, after being released by the Mets in spring training that year], there's that connection with Billy Martin and the Texas Rangers, and we turned around that franchise. Hitting, stealing, running, getting hit by the ball - we were playing "Billy Ball." So Billy Ball was innate to me, that was how we played in college - we ran, bunted, stole, squeezed, got signs…we did whatever it took to win. And then the Yankees called me on Thurman Munson's tragic day, unfortunately. It was like *a morgue* walking into the clubhouse [which would have been probably August 3rd - the day after Munson's passing] - George Steinbrenner was very polite, Tommy John, Luis Tiant, Bucky Dent, they were all like, "Hey man. We're all out of it right now. This is tragic. We don't believe this is happening. The guy crashed in a plane."

I was thinking of Koosman, because I knew Koosman would fly to Minnesota, and I'm going, "Man, maybe I ought to tell Kooz to cool it on days off." Everybody started thinking about their welfare, because athletes don't think about dying and death - the thing about "the next meal" and "the next hit" and "the next win." But when that happened…Piniella just lost it, and Nettles. And I'm going, "Lou, it's going to be alright." "No, man. You don't know, you don't know." I had talked to Thurman prior - as a Texas Ranger - a lot, joking, before I hit. I'd get in the box, and go, "OK. Who's calling the game today - Thurman or you, Nestor [Chylak, a longtime American League umpire]?" There was a kind of camaraderie around and respect that we had for Thurman as a captain. I mean, umpires would go, "Heck, if he's calling the game, *it's going to be a quick game.*"

MIKE TORREZ: With the Yankees [who Torrez played for in 1977], all the tradition that they've had through the years - all the championships that they won - being a Yankee, it was a great, great feeling, when we won in '77 [Torrez was 2-0 in the '77 Word Series, and was the winning pitcher in the Series-winning Game 6, which is best remembered for Reggie Jackson's three home runs]. It was good, it's a New York team - it had the Mets, and the Mets were building up their tradition.

LENNY RANDLE: You ever heard of rock stars like the Beatles? The Yankees had an entourage all the time. Going to the airport was 20,000 people and getting to your car was 5,000 or 10,000 people - as a Yankee. It was just that intense. On the road - Kansas City, Minnesota, wherever we went - it was like a rock group was traveling. I'm like, *"Wow.* It's like a World Series going on just to go to the bathroom!" It was amazing. So, being a Met, it was a little more low key, because there was no line at 4:00 coming to the stadium. At Yankee Stadium, there would be maybe 4,000 to 5,000 people at Yankee Stadium, whereas there may have been 1,000 or 200 at Shea Stadium, pre-game.

      And then the pre-game Met people get off the train, and getting out of the car was not as intense to get in the clubhouse and locker room as it was at Yankee Stadium - you had to have a guard or security. It was major hype for a lot of the players. With the Mets, when they hired Torre, it picked up more, and then when Seaver left...it kept fluctuating. And then when Flynn and Henderson and Youngblood and all the "new group" came in, it picked up again. Because Dougie Flynn was like a rock star - with the hair. He did things outside the box - he was a creative guy, and still is! He probably had a 5,000 to 10,000 "poster-boy fan base" or something - groupies or old grandmas that love hair. [Laughs]

PAT ZACHRY: Yeah, we took some heat for that - if both teams had been winning, with a chance of meeting down the line, it would have been a lot different. But they were so far superior to what we had, and that was not only hard to live with, it was hard to listen to. Because we took a lot of the bad vibes off of that. But hey, if you're losing, you're losing. Nothing's ever easy when you're losing - it doesn't matter where you're playing.

JOHN STEARNS: It didn't bother me at all. I took one game at a time. I came from Denver, I grew up playing wiffle ball in my backyard with my brothers, and we had baseball cards, line-ups, stacked up - American League vs. National League - in the late '50s/early '60s. I was watching baseball out of Denver, Colorado, and for me to play major league baseball in New York City was a thrill beyond description. A kid that came out of Denver, just to be there was an honor for me, and it was way higher than my expectations. You can't really be twelve years old and living in Denver and think that some day, you're going to play major league baseball in New York City. That's too big of a step forward. And for me to be able to do that, it's been a privilege and an honor. And so much fun.

CHAPTER 26:
VS.

CHARLIE PULEO: Montreal had a really good club in those years. Al Oliver, Gary Carter, Andre Dawson, Tim Raines - they were tough. And the Pirates were really good - Dave Parker, Bill Madlock. They were tough to pitch against. That whole era, the National League was a pretty good league. The Dodgers had a good line-up. And Joe Torre with the Braves were winning the Nation League West - with Dale Murphy and Chris Chambliss and that whole crew down there.

PETE FALCONE: I always thought the Expos had the best team in the division. I still - to this day - say they should have won the division. In '79 they should have won the division, in '80. I just thought they had the best all-around line-up - this is coming from a left-hand pitcher standpoint, my opinion. Other guys would say no. But you look at that outfield they had, they had great pitchers - they had Steve Rogers, Charlie Lea, and Bill Gullickson. Those were any best top three starters in the league.

And that line-up that they had - Gary Carter catching, hitting, Andre Dawson was the most feared hitter in the league at the time, I thought. Him and Ellis Valentine, Warren Cromartie, Larry Parish, and Gary Carter. That's a good line-up right there. Tim Raines came, and Tim Wallach - another great home run hitter. They had the best team, in my opinion. Now, I don't know why they didn't win it, what happened, if they had injuries. But, of course, the Phillies most of the time edged them out, and Pittsburgh did. I don't know how they did that, because I would rather face the Phillies, Pirates, Cardinals, or Reds any time over the Expos.

JEFF REARDON: Montreal [was the best team of the era]. And we never won. '81, we got to the playoffs and go to that Game 5 against the Dodgers, and we were all set to play the Yankees in the World Series if we won. The only game the manager didn't put me in to close it out, he put Steve Rogers in. I was actually warming up next to him. I thought it was a mistake, because [Expos manager] Jim Fanning had made me the closer when Dick Williams got fired. Because Dick would not give me the ball to close games, and management was getting mad at him, and finally, they fired his ass. And then Fanning, when he took over, he introduced himself, and said, "I'm going to be the manager, and you're going to be my closer the rest of the way." It went good - I helped get them into the playoffs.

     We were expected to be "the team of the '80s," with the players we had. I think by losing Game 5, that just did us in. I think if we had gotten to the Series, they would have seen us a couple more times. It was that big of a crush. And I guess I struck out Rick Monday four out of five times that year [Monday hit a go-ahead solo home run in the bottom of the 9th inning off Rogers, which would be the difference - the Dodgers beat the Expos, 2-1, to advance to the 1981 World Series, and eventually, beat the Yankees in six games]. Today, that wouldn't happen - everything is computerized. I didn't even know it - I didn't know it until I retired, because some writer called up, and said, "Did you realize you faced Monday like, four times and struck him out all four times?" And I said, "Well, I remember I wasn't too worried about facing him." And that's why I was shocked he brought in Steve Rogers.

     But Steve was the "Tom Seaver of Montreal," and they probably wanted to give him a chance to close it out. I thought he was warming up for the first game of the World Series! Because he had a beard, the umpire comes out, does the thing - wipes his face like the guy with the beard. Well, we've both got a beard. He just walked in and, "No Jeff, not you." I said, *"Are you sure?"* Because Steve had never pitched in relief. He goes, "Yeah, he said Rogers." And Steve gave up that home run to lose the game. And then after that, we were second place a lot, but we should have won some World Series. I mean, that was the best team I ever saw. We had superstars coming out of our...one year, I was leading the league in saves, and the league told me I couldn't make [the All-Star team], because they had five All-Stars! That's the excuse they gave me. Of course, I think it was Tommy Lasorda wanted his boy out there - Steve Howe - instead of me.

CRAIG SWAN: The mid '70s, it was definitely the Cincinnati Reds, and they were good until '77/'78. And then the Pirates started getting good - the "We Are Family" team, with Willie Stargell and all those guys. They were all such good players. Pete Rose hit me like a drum, Dave Parker was an awful good hitter, Dave Winfield was a great hitter when he was with San Diego, Steve Garvey and Ron Cey, the Dodgers, and the Phillies had Mike Schmidt and Greg Luzinski, and St. Louis had Bake McBride, Keith Hernandez, and Ted Simmons. Each team had their great players, and it was fun pitching against them.

JOHN STEARNS: Nolan Ryan was really good - I was able to hit him a little bit. But the guy that was the hardest to hit off of - being a right-hand hitter - was Kent Tekulve, the side-armed closer for the Pittsburgh Pirates. He threw about 93 from down under, on the right hand side, and his fastball would just dive in on you. It was a sinker ball coming back in on the right hander's fists. And then, from the side-arm delivery, he would change to a slider, which was going away from the right-handed hitter. And his control, I was just waiting for him to give me something to hit out over the plate, but he would throw that sinker right in on the inside corner. He never had the ball out at a good spot to hit. And for a right handed hitter, to try to figure out how to hit a fastball that's coming in on your fists - as opposed to a slider - from that down under delivery point, going away from you, he was just really a hard guy to hit for a right handed hitter.

The best team out of those years was probably the Phillies - they just had the whole package over there. They had some veteran players, and some younger guys, like Larry Christenson, Dick Ruthven, Lonnie Smith. And they had some veteran players that were really good players, like Pete Rose, Mike Schmidt, Bob Boone, Greg Luzinski, Garry Maddox was tremendous, they also had Bake McBride over there. They had a good team, and they had people coming off the bench that could hit, and then their pitching staff, with Steve Carlton, and Tug McGraw was the closer, Larry Christenson and Dick Ruthven pitching...wow, what a team. When you asked that question, I went right to the Phillies.

JERRY KOOSMAN: Certainly Pittsburgh was one tough club to play against. The Dodgers had Ron Cey and Steve Garvey. Gosh, you can go right around the league - St. Louis had Gibson and Brock and Curt Flood, Chicago had Ernie Banks, Billy Williams, and Ron Santo, Cincinnati early on had individual players - Pete Rose - but maybe the club wasn't as a whole as strong. Gosh, Atlanta had Aaron, Joe Torre, Frisco had Juan Marichal, Willie McCovey, and Willie Mays, Philadelphia had Richie Allen. There were some big names around.

WALT TERRELL: Oh Lord, there's so many players. The best teams, well, the '84 Cubs, they were awfully damned good. Really, really good. And I remember the Dodgers were good - not that the other teams weren't, it's just right off the top of the head. The Dodgers, always with the pitching, pitching, pitching. But boy, the Cubs that year were, wow, they were really, really good. They had good pitching, too. That '84 group was a pretty special group, and I think those Cubs would say the same thing.

The Cardinals those years were always good. I know there was some flak in '82, because the Mets pitched some of us younger guys that came up and there was a pennant race going on, and teams bitched, "What are you doing pitching these rookie guys?" I pitched my first game, and hell, they're in a pennant race. Scared to death, but excited at the same time. Very fortunate to have gotten to pitch against them.

Players, Dave Parker - what a talent. I was fortunate to pitch against some of the guys that I grew up with, who were my heroes - a bunch of the Reds. I grew up not too far from Cincinnati, Ohio, so those things. And the Dale Murphys of the world. The Steve Garveys, the Tony Gwynns - those type of guys. The Mike Schmidts of the world, the Greg Luzinskis, and the Larry Bowas. Very fortunate to have the opportunity to pitch against those people.

RICK OWNBEY: One of my tough outs that stuck out for me was Dale Murphy. If I pitched him in, he ripped it down the left field line. If I pitched him away, he hit it over the right center field wall. There was a time when that guy was obviously very tough.

RANDY JONES: The late '70s, the Phillies were always tough, and St. Louis. That west coast swing would always be tough on us - with the Mets. Lord, we didn't dominate. We fared pretty well, but we'd lose two out of three to the Dodgers and then the Giants, the Padres, we'd handle that.

STEVE HENDERSON: I played against some pretty good teams in St. Louis and Pittsburgh. In that time, we had a lot of good teams to play against - Montreal, all of them.

DAN NORMAN: I faced JR Richards, and him heating it up there pretty good - like, *real good.* The Niekro brothers [Phil and Joe], both Niekros were throwing good with the knuckle ball. That's tough to hit. Pete Rose was still playing. And the Dodgers had a good organization, with Garvey and all those guys there. There were still a lot of good ball players playing during that time in the late '70s.

PAT ZACHRY: Off the top of my head, Willie Stargell. Not only was he a great player, he was just a first-class gentleman - on and off the field, always, 24/7. Garvey was another one, Schmidt. You may not like it, but you've got to admit Pete was. A guy like Randy Jones - who was later on, a teammate. It was an interesting time to be a player.

BRENT GAFF: I was always in awe with Pete Rose, because I heard so much about him growing up. But I don't think he ever got a hit off me - I think he was 0-9 against me or something like that. But the one guy that I couldn't get a ball by was Steve Garvey. I'd get him down 0-2, and nibble the shit off the plate, and he'd foul it off, foul it off, foul it off, and then sooner or later, I'd beat him and get in on him, and he'd hit it off the end of the bat and bloop it over the infield! I couldn't get him out.

I told Mel [Stottlemyre, who joined the Mets as their pitching coach in 1984], "OK Mel, how in the hell am I going to get this son of a bitch out? No matter what I do, he spoils all my good pitches until he gets me so where I've got to throw a strike. And then he ends up hitting it." And Mel says, "Believe me, this will work on him - just throw a batting practice speed fastball right down the middle, with nothing on it. About pecker high." And I said, "Are you shitting me?" And he said, "Yeah, those veterans, their eyes light up when they see that shit." I tried it, and sure enough, he popped it up to the second baseman. It took a lot of short hairs to do that.

But then after that though, I went to winter ball when I was doing really well, and I tried to do that against Andrés Galarraga with the bases loaded and two out, and thought, "Well, this kid is making sawdust out of the handle." He was a rookie - he wasn't even in the big leagues yet. He was batting cleanup, and I knew he'd be swinging for the fences, so I threw him one of those pecker highs, and he hit a bullet off the centerfield wall, and three runs scored! So I knew after that, it don't work on rookies - it only works on veterans. But I would say Garvey was the toughest.

TOM GORMAN: Mike Schmidt would have to be up there. I had a really good career against Schmidty. He hit a triple off me the last time I faced him - he almost took my head off, it hit about a foot from going out at dead center at Veterans Stadium. But I bet I struck him out six times prior to that. I also saw him carry games - he was so good. He was probably the best all-around player that I ever played against.

And then you've got to throw Tony Gwynn in there. I played with Tony the last part of my career [in 1987] - Tony Gwynn was the greatest hitter I have ever seen. To give you an idea of just how sharp that guy was, I struck him out in '84 on a pitch that was maybe a foot-and-a-half outside and a foot low. [The umpire] missed it, and it was a strike three. I was amazed, and obviously, Tony was amazed. So that was in '84. Well, I come into spring training in '87 in Yuma, and the first guy I run into is Tony Gwynn. I put my hand out and say, "Tom Gorman," he says, "Tony Gwynn...*it was a ball.*" But he only struck out like 24 times that year! Think about that - five hundred and something at-bats and he only struck out 24 times. That's amazing. So I would have to say Gwynn, for sure.

Ryne Sandberg was there too at that time, and he was a fantastic player. He's a northwest boy - he went to Spokane, here. And then to watch Nolan Ryan in the latter part of his career still deal - that was pretty impressive, too.

226 The Seventh Year Stretch

Ryan would strikeout fourteen men before you opened your eyes. I saw him one night against a pretty darn good Expos team, the first guy to foul one off was Tim Wallach, and he batted sixth. So that gives you an idea of how he was throwing that night.

And I'd have to throw Keith in there - he was as good a player as anybody in that era. He ripped it up. And you've go to throw Gary in there, too. I mean, Gary will probably go down in history as one of the greatest catchers of all-time. It's sad that he passed [in 2012 at the age of 57], because nobody would have appreciated going to all these Hall of Fame deals than Gary would have. And that's really the saddest part - other than leaving his family - he would have just enjoyed the shit out of all of those ceremonies and stuff.

JEFF REARDON: I never had trouble with righties, but Dusty Baker was very tough on me, for a right-handed hitter. And Pete Rose I would say was the toughest left-hander on me. And the pitchers, you still had guys like Ryan, JR Richards - I'm talking early '80s. And of course, Seaver. Ryan, and Richards' speed impressed me the most, and Seaver the command of all his pitches.

LENNY RANDLE: I liked facing all of them. The whole staff of St. Louis I loved - I would wear them out! I didn't mind facing anybody. It didn't matter - there was no staff to me that dominated our line-up. With a hitter's point of view, I never had a problem - because of Ted Williams. That was my first major league manager [with the Washington Senators in 1971 and Texas Rangers in 1972]. There was nothing intimidating. He'd say, *"You're the intimidator. Never give a pitcher that much credit to get you out. You're getting yourself out."* So having him as a mentor and as a hitting coach and a manager and off-the-field/on-the-field kind of guy, for as long as he was alive, he would check on us. "OK, you need to do this, you need to do that." And we would listen. We were a sponge.

MIKE TORREZ: Back then, who was tough…Jesus, *everybody* was tough. [Laughs] Once you're in the major leagues, every hitter, you've got to work your butt off to get hitters out. Back then, you had to battle really every game. There was never really an easy win. There was never a "give me" - put it that way. Not in major league baseball. You've got to earn what the hell you got.

CRAIG SWAN: People ask me, "What do I miss the most about baseball?" I miss facing the hitter. That was a true challenge.

CHAPTER 27:
HERNANDEZ =
HALL OF FAME?

TIM McCARVER: Yes, I do. I think anybody who adds a new dimension of playing his position - Jim Kaat did it as a pitcher, winning 16 gold gloves. It's a new dimension. Plus, he pitched 26 years. And I would talk about them in the same breath. Because Kitty [Kaat's nickname] added a new dimension to fielding his position, and of course, a 20 game winner many times over - two 20 game seasons with the White Sox, and his longevity. And Keith did the same thing. He just opened your eyes as to how first base could - and should - be played.

STEVE JACOBSON: I voted for him until he ran out of time. I used to write a column on my Hall of Fame ballot, and I said, "This is a throwaway vote, because the people in Minneapolis who never saw him play - and just saw his numbers - wouldn't vote for him." But he belonged in the Hall of Fame. And at the time, Hernandez was coming off a drug issue with the Cardinals, and the Cardinals wanted to get rid of him. He had been the Most Valuable Player...or shared it [in 1979, with Willie Stargell]. Cashen had Neil Allen, which was the trade - which made it a hell of a bargain. But Cashen lingered over that trade for a couple of days, because he wasn't sure about the drug issue. And I remember Hernandez's first year with the Mets, going to lunch with Cashen and several other writers, and he asked each of us to write on a piece of paper who we thought was the Most Valuable Player. And I don't remember who I picked and who the other guys picked, but Cashen turned up his ballot, and it was Hernandez.

And a terrific interview. I remember talking with him about drugs in baseball, and why it was such an important issue for baseball. He said, "Because you could control the World Series." If you had a player who was doing hard drugs - like cocaine - and you were a gambler, and you offered to give this player enough cocaine to get him through seven games of the World Series, essentially two weeks. Keith said, "No. It would be gone after three days, and the player would be of no use to you at all. He would use it all."

Hernandez had so much going for him - as a personality on the team. And, when he was traded to the Mets, he cried in the locker room. He didn't want to come to New York, because New York was too busy, too menacing for him. He said, "New York would be a rest stop" - he would essentially have dinner and go to his hotel. And later, he told me it was so different in New York. In St. Louis, people thought that they owned the players - the fans. And he would go to dinner in a restaurant, and the fans would not let him have any peace. He said, "If you go to a good restaurant in New York, people would look at you and they might nod, but they would leave you alone."

JERRY KOOSMAN: Sure. There's a lot of guys I can think of that I'd like to see in the Hall of Fame. I've been part of a group that's been trying to get Gil Hodges in the Hall of Fame, but that's not working out too well, either.

RANDY JONES: Sure, I think he does. I look at players, and I'm big on what kind of impact did they make on baseball. I think Keith Hernandez did make an impact on baseball. I think deservedly so [Hernandez belongs in the Hall of Fame]. Sooner or later, I would hope that he would get into the Hall of Fame.

DAN NORMAN: I know he led the league in hitting one year, and he was the co-MVP with Willie Stargell. Yeah, I think he does. I was looking at some stats one night, and Minnie Miñoso...*he had some stats!* I'm like, "This guy's not in the Hall of Fame, in all the years he played and the numbers he put up?" And the reason I looked him up is he had passed recently [on March 1, 2015, at the age of 89]. But like I was talking to one of my brothers, we were talking sports, and I think when you have the fans voting for the All-Star Game, they can stuff the ballot. Before, it used to be the players voting. So if the players were voting for the Hall of Fame, I think those guys would be in it. But now, they have the writers voting. So the writers have different decisions - they don't see a guy every day like the players do. So their opinion is going to be a lot different. It makes a difference when the writers are putting you in compared to the players putting you in. But those guys were good - they'd get my vote.

JOHN STEARNS: Keith probably had 2,000 hits, maybe 200 home runs, maybe 1,200 or 1,300 RBI's. Am I right with that? Am I close? [Hernandez finished his career with 2,182 hits, 162 home runs, 1,071 RBI's, and a batting average of .296] They're probably looking for more home runs out of a guy like him. Keith hit for average - I think he's a guy that certainly can be a Hall of Famer, no doubt. But he didn't have 300 home runs, he probably didn't drive in 1,500 runs. It's stat-driven, a lot of it, and he's probably short in a couple of areas.

Yet, when you put him on the defensive side of the ball, he's as good as anybody that ever played over there. Did he play 20 years? I don't know. [Hernandez played 17 seasons, from 1974-1990] Those are borderline numbers, but if you just go by numbers, there are other things to take in consideration. And he certainly was as good a first baseman that has ever played [Hernandez won eleven consecutive Gold Glove Awards, from 1978-1988]. He brought energy to the park every day and played on a lot of winning teams. A great player, no doubt. Did he have Hall of Fame numbers? It's marginal. But there are some factors to consider.

MIKE TORREZ: Did he put the numbers up? If you have to ask me "If somebody belongs in the Hall of Fame," then apparently, they don't. For defensive purposes, yes. Keith's a good friend of mine, and Keith was one of the best first basemen fielding-wise there ever was in the game. Average, he didn't hit a lot of home runs - he was more of a "line drive hitter." I would say he's borderline, right on the fence. He definitely helped the Mets in their glory years to win.

GARY "BABA BOOEY" DELL'ABATE: That's a good question. Here's the thing - probably stat-wise, he doesn't. But there are intangibles, like I don't think the Mets win in '86 without him on the field. I just think that he was so important to the team. Let me look at the numbers here…he's got 2,100 hits. That's not going to get you in. He's got 162 home runs. But he was MVP, went to All-Star games - he's right on the border.

　　　But again, for me, the answer is "Yes," because I love him. And I do think his importance as a smart baseball player sort of managing the team on the field, that's an intangible that a lot of people don't take into account. I think a lot of times, people just look at the stats on paper. Listen, I think Bill Buckner should be in the Hall of Fame. I think if that ball doesn't go through his legs [in Game 6 of the 1986 World Series], he's in the Hall of Fame. What is he, like 2,700/2,800 hits? [Buckner finished his career with 2,715 hits] It's a very subjective thing.

JEFF REARDON: Possibly. I don't think he's a sure Hall of Famer, but I would put him in my class, because I'm never going to get there - a guy that really should have gotten a better chance to make it.

BRENT GAFF: I'll tell you what, I've never seen anybody better when the game's on the line. It was just amazing. You weren't beating him, if he had a chance to win the game for you. Some of the stuff that I'd seen him do was amazing. I'd never seen anybody play first base like that. If you ever watched him in warm-ups or during the game, if he's throwing to second base to start a double play, it's chest-high, right where it needs to be - every time, no matter where he's throwing it from. And the stuff that he picked over there at first...I don't know, I think a lot of this Hall of Fame stuff, you've got to stick around for a long time and stay healthy.

TOM GORMAN: I don't believe there was a better first baseman that played first base than Keith. Now, they're not going to go off of that - they just aren't. He was a Gold Glove winner eleven times, so that shows you what the rest of the league thought of him. And he'd play out of position so far and he'd get the ball, and you'd have to bust your ass to get to first to cover, because that was a second baseman's ball that Keith's stealing, because he knew the hitter so well.

So if you were going to go strictly on what he was as a fielder - which is probably the best in that stretch at first base than anybody - and if you went on the fact that he went on 2,400 hits or whatever [2,182 hits] and 1,000 or so RBI's [1,071 RBI's], I don't think there was a better first baseman in the league at that period of time. People would argue that maybe Garvey was over there at first with the Dodgers, but I'm trying to think of another guy that would have been that good at that position...there just wasn't. He was the best at that position. To sum it up, they're not going to put him in because he didn't hit .300 [he hit .296], he didn't have 3,000 this. But of all the tangibles, of being a first baseman, and all the things that he did for that team, I'd have him in there.

RANDY JONES: I have no argument with that, my friend [In response to me saying that if Ozzie Smith is in the Hall of Fame - who finished his career with a .262 batting average and thirteen consecutive Gold Glove Awards - then there is no reason why Hernandez shouldn't be in the Hall of Fame, too]. Ozzie probably got into the Hall of Fame because he could do a cartwheel and a somersault. [Laughs] That was pretty unique there all by itself. Year in and year out, how he played first base and the clutch hits that he got - I don't see any argument in that, my friend.

TOM GORMAN: Well, Oz went in the Hall of Fame for the same reason I'd say Keith should - because there wasn't a better shortstop in that period of time in baseball, to do what they did. Field the ball and play the position the way it's supposed to be played, and obviously, Keith helped a young pitching staff develop into a great pitching staff. I would definitely give Keith the praise - he's in *my* Hall of Fame, let's put it that way.

GARY "BABA BOOEY" DELL'ABATE: But the problem with Ozzie Smith is his fielding so overshadows everything. And it's hard to be a flashy first baseman. It's easier to be a flashy shortstop.

MIKE FITZGERALD: There's a lot of guys that just play and have that kind of "travel ball mentality," where they go 3-4 and they're singing in the showers when you lose 5-4. Keith wasn't that way. Keith wanted to win, he wanted to play well, and he was willing to encourage and motivate his teammates. I really respected that about him.

STEVE ZABRISKIE: I do. Without question. I know that the writers guard what they call the integrity of the Hall of Fame very judiciously. And very fervently. But I believe that there are occasions when they do it to a fault. And I believe that they - and I don't know this for a fact, because

I'm not a member of the Baseball Writer's Association, I respect those guys, I think they do a wonderful job and many of them are super talented - but as a group, I think they've made some poor choices in their stance. And I'll just have to call it "a stance" - their position or whatever you want to call it - on who they let in and who they don't.

I think that they've kind of thrown a blanket over a situation here and have not been willing to or able to consider individual circumstances enough, to make decisions. They've taken what I believe is the easy way out, by saying, "If this, then this." And they've created maybe a formula to make it easy for themselves to take an overall position - regardless of the individual. I don't think that's fair. I don't think it's right. And I think the Hall of Fame should be bigger than that. I don't know, and I can't accuse or speak to it with any degree of certainty, but I have to assume that Keith Hernandez has been lumped into the group. And I don't think that's right. I don't think it's right for him and I don't think it's right for some other people. But my opinion doesn't really matter. But I do feel strongly that he should be in, and I feel strongly that there are others that should be in. And I think that in trying to preserve whatever it is they feel the sanctity of the Hall of Fame is, I think they're doing baseball a disservice.

CHAPTER 28:
TODAY

GARY "BABA BOOEY" DELL'ABATE: I'm in my 31st year of producing 'The Howard Stern Show,' and I'm in my 54th year of being a Met fan.

PETE FALCONE: I live in Louisiana. I moved here 20 years ago, to coach a minor league baseball team. After I finished playing ball, I made a few comebacks - I even went one year to play baseball in Italy, which was a lot of fun. And then I came here in '94, to live in Central Louisiana, to coach a minor league team. And then I coached college. So as time has gone on and raising a family, you don't have that money coming in, so you've got to recreate yourself. That's what I've had to do. And face life. As the years have gone on, I've become a certified chef - I'm a pretty good chef here in Louisiana. I'm in food service right now, and that's what I like to do.

Last year, I came to New York for Memorial Day, and they had my son Joseph throw out the first ball, and they had "US Serviceman Night" [at Citi Field]. My son was a corpsman in Afghanistan and Iraq, with the Marines. So it was a good story - the kid comes back from war, and the next thing you know, he's playing baseball for Columbia University. So they picked up on that and made a big deal of Joseph. And he threw the first ball out at the Yankee/Mets game last year on Memorial Day. I was there on the field, and it was exciting. But that's the only time I've been to Citi Field. I think Citi Field is one of the nicest stadiums I've ever seen. I love that place. It was so whimsical. Beautiful stadium.

I would love to get involved in this time of my life in some Mets Fantasy Camps. I would like to do that - why not? But they don't contact me. I'm not even alive to them. That's how   it   goes   in   life.

MIKE FITZGERALD: I've been coaching youth baseball since I left spring training in '94, and I've also been coaching at the high school level off and on, which I'm on right now - this will be my last year in my tour of duty. But I've been coaching youth baseball, trying to be a good influence on young players, and also, just as important, coaches. That's what I've been doing, and to make a living, I've been working as an insurance agent here in Southern California. I'm an independent agent, so I'm writing cars, houses, properties, umbrellas, boats, and motorcycles.

BRENT GAFF: I'm about retired. I've had a construction company [Gaffight Home Improvement] - windows, siding, remodeling, roofing, stuff like that - for the last almost 30 years. And I don't really have to work very hard at that anymore - I just pick and choose what jobs I want.

I've got a little thing called Gaffight Custom Rods - I make custom fishing rods. And I sell lots of them. If you ever look at iceshanty.com, my stuff is highly sought after. I make a lot of money in my shop - I've got a shop here at my house, and I sell...not a whole lot, as many as I want to make though. I really have no bills, everything I've got is paid for. My wife sells real estate, and we're comfortable. We're not rich by no means. We've got 20 acres and a house - 12 acres of it's woods. It's kind of set back in the woods. Here in Indiana, where I'm surrounded by over a thousand lakes, so ice fishing is real big. So I build ice fishing rods in the winter, and then I'll do fly rods and steelhead rods in the summer, just for spending money.

And I do get a little pension from the Mets that I'm going to start drawing here one of these days. I could have drawn it a long time ago - it's worth enough where I should be alright after I retire. I think I'm going to start drawing it when I'm 60. Y'know, I've made custom Mets rods, with all the colors, and make rods for some of the old players. Tom Gorman, I just made him a rod yesterday, for steelhead. If you look at Gaffight Custom Rods on the Internet, we do some pretty nice work, me and my son. Both my boys pitched their way through school - until both of them blew their arms out. But both of them were probably going to get drafted - they were both scouted pretty heavy.

TOM GORMAN: I work for a company, Lids Team Sports. We're a national company - we sell sporting equipment and uniforms. Mainly Nike uniforms to colleges and high schools in my area. This is the first year in a long time where I'm not coaching - I just took the year off from coaching. I've been coaching some high school as a pitching coach. But I do some individual pitching instruction for young kids. But mainly, I've been doing this for 20 years or so. Sherwood, Oregon, is our home, which is just south of Portland, Oregon. All our kids are grown up, so the wife and I moved into a condo and just kind of downsized from the house. Mainly just playing golf and working - trying to play as much golf as I can.

STEVE HENDERSON: Right now, I am the hitting coach for the Philadelphia Phillies.

STEVE JACOBSON: I wrote a book about compulsive gambling ['All Bets Are Off']. And I like baseball - I go to baseball games, I watch. I lament the pace that they have imposed on the game. A long ballgame should be a good game - but you get a lot of long ballgames that are not good games.

There's a book around that you may have seen, called '501 Baseball Books Fans Must Read Before They Die,' and I'm #206 with 'Carrying Jackie's Torch.' I thought that was a terrible job by the publisher - it came out in

February of the year the Hall of Fame inducted like, 21 black players, and they never even offered the book to bookstores in Cooperstown or the bookstore at the Hall of Fame. I'm forever infuriated by a book that I thought should have been sold as the American experience or the black experience, or growing up in America, and the role of the black player, but they never touched it. So I'm still pissed about that!

RANDY JONES: I'm still working for the ballclub here, the Padres, in the public relations department. And pre-game and post-game radio, and a little pre-game TV. I'm not traveling anymore with the team, I'm kind of a homebody - just staying here in San Diego and enjoying my grandkids. I have BBQ stands at Petco Park ["Randy Jones BBQ"] - this will be my 23rd year. You might say I'm the "Boog Powell of San Diego" - Boog started his a year before I did, and then I jumped on the bandwagon and started my BBQ in I think it was '93 or '94. And I've been doing that every year, as well. It keeps me around the fans, and I enjoy doing that.

JERRY KOOSMAN: Just staying warm! It was five below this morning, so when it's cold, I pretty much stay in the house and do a lot of reading on the Internet, and watch golf on TV, and certainly football in the fall. And I have a Border Collie that's a great friend and pet. And I play cards - I like to play bridge and Euchre, and I do that through the winter, also. It's a relaxing retired life, I guess. I live about 50   miles   north   east   of   Minneapolis.

SKIP LOCKWOOD: I'm going to play golf today. I'm writing my own book. My wife published her book a few years ago ['Major League Bride: An Inside Look at Life Outside the Ballpark' by Kathleen Lockwood], so I'm in the process of writing mine. It will be more about an inside look at baseball rather than a memoir or something like that. We will see if I have the ambition to get that out the door one of these days. It might be interesting to have a player write a book that people can read, that takes them on the field and inside the action, as opposed to having someone else write about the player. If I can write it well enough, I can actually take the person with me on the field - that's what I'm trying to do.

TIM McCARVER: I did 30 games with the Cardinals last year, I'm doing 40 games this year [2015], and it's kind of full circle for me. I signed with the Cardinals in 1959, came up with up the Cardinals in '59, played thirteen years with St. Louis - about twelve of those thirteen years I was in the big leagues, only one year in the minors. But I'm back to where I was "born," so if there is ever a full circle in baseball, I think I am an example of that. And I'm very happy as a result.

DAN NORMAN: I work for a junior college - Barstow College. I coached a team there for about eight years, and now I have another position, I work in M&O - maintenance and operations with the college. Still doing some baseball camps when they call me. I just had my second hip replacement, and I'm looking to retire from the college in a couple more years.

RICK OWNBEY: When I got out of the game of baseball, that #1 question that a lot of us have is, "Now what do I do?" Strangely enough, I ended up going down to the beach, and met some people that played "two men in the sand" - beach volleyball. And I said, "Wow, that looks interesting." One thing led to another, and I started to pick the game up. And if you think about it, when you throw a baseball, the arm swing for hitting a volleyball is very similar. So I did actually play a little of the AVP - Association of Volleyball Professionals - and played in all the California pro events after I got out of ball, for about five years.

I live out in Fallbrook, California, and I've got a two-acre property here. I do work for a company called SportsForce Recruiting - we assist families with student/athletes to help them get into the right colleges, with hopefully some scholarship money. I think we all are aware that the cost of schooling is out of control.

And I also do a lot of caretaking or housesitting. A lot of these people have four or five acres and horses and dogs and cats, and they may leave seven to ten days at a time, and I will take on their properties while they're gone. And then also we have a self-serve fruit stand out here, that we run every Friday, Saturday, and Sunday, and if Monday's a holiday, we'll run it four. So with the two acres, I have a tremendous amount of avocados and a lot of fruit trees, and the guy who lives across the street has been out here about 40 years, and they have eleven acres, and he's always had this fruit stand. And since I've been out here - for about ten years - it's done nothing but grow. And my wife and I have got two dogs and five cats, so I'm plenty busy - that's for sure!

CHARLIE PULEO: I've been coaching a high school team - I live in Tennessee. I've coached there for about ten years. I coached in the minor leagues with the Baltimore Orioles for seven years, up in Bloomfield, West Virginia. Right now, I'm still teaching at the high school. I gave up the baseball coaching, but we do a radio show - we do a sports page on Saturday mornings on a local station here in town, and we cover the University of Tennessee sports and local college, and high school - we do a whole hour on high school sports. We've been doing it for three or four years. It's a good hobby for us - myself and two other guys that are retired. That keeps me in sports, and I've got a couple of years until I retire.

LENNY RANDLE: I am a global general manager of Nettuno-Anzio, Italian baseball league. I've been doing it nine years, and I'm just trying to find the next Mike Piazza or Joe DiMaggio or Roy Campanella. I'm doing a couple of songs with a record label to bring funds and sponsor a youth sports and education in Italy and internationally in America. We've given out about 375,000 scholarships, and they're free. So I'm thinking I can find an international bond with education and sports and music, to have those kids over there come here.

We had a kid signed, Federico Giordani, and he got about $375,000 from the Dodgers. He could be...I don't want put that tag of "DiMaggio" on him yet, because it's a mental, everyday playing thing. It used to be we'd play a 40-50 game schedule, now it's down to like a 20 game schedule with two games a week. So I'm trying to get the league back to how it was with sponsors and donations and enthusiasm for the game - like we have here in America. And it's slowly, gradually happening. We're doing a documentary for the MLB Network about that.

JEFF REARDON: Today, I'm just hanging around, doing nothing. I don't work anymore. I do autograph shows, but there hasn't been too many of those lately. I follow the game very close on the Internet. I still love the game. I would have loved to get a nice front office job, but you've got to go through the minor leagues to get all that stuff, and I'm not doing that. I did that once, and I feel I can recognize talent real good. But you don't get those kinds of jobs too often.

JOHN STEARNS: Actually, this is my first year [2015] I'm kind of semi-retired. I'm 63. I've been in baseball since 1973, so I've got 42 years in baseball. I've been coaching, managing, playing, and scouting in professional baseball for 42 years. I'm not going to spring training this year - I'm thinking I might be retired here. I'm so lucky - I've got the major league pension, I've got the minor league pension, I've got social security. Financially, it's not a problem to not work anymore. The last five years, I've been with the Seattle Mariners. Before that, I worked for probably half a dozen teams since I quit playing - as a minor league manager, a major league coach, a professional scout...I've just been all over the place.

CRAIG SWAN: After doing rolfing for 28 years up in Connecticut, I needed to retire, because the rolfing technique that I used to help people with bad necks and bad backs and hip problems was very tough on me. It was a very strenuous job, and I've created some neck issues, which I get rolfed for, which takes care of the pain, but if I rolf too much now, my neck locks up on me, because it's like doing a weight workout - to work on people.

So I've retired from that, and I am now flying radio-controlled aircrafts for the Collier Fun Flyers, down in Naples, three days a week, about four hours a day. About 35 guys that are much older than me - we have some 92 years old - and we fly radio-controlled aircrafts. I build and fly now, and it's mainly what I do, besides work around the house and do what my wife tells me to do. [Laughs]

I'm an avid radio controlled enthusiast. I am working on my planes maybe five or six hours a day. It's a lot of fun, it takes a lot of skill, there's been a lot of crashes, and some near injuries, but nobody's actually been injured. But it takes a lot of skill - it's almost like a videogame, but real life, as far as you have to move your fingers to control your plane. So I enjoy it. It takes me back to my childhood, when my dad was working for the aviation companies back in Southern California, with Douglas and North American he worked for, and we did a lot of aircraft stuff, so I'm kind of going back to my childhood I think. It's fun to build something that can fly and land and take off.

WALT TERRELL: I today am the grandfather of four, and I work for Pepsi Cola out of Cincinnati - been doing that, gosh, 20 years now. I coached high school baseball for

20 years, and I have a summer baseball program that's in its 22nd year [the Kentucky Colonels]. I don't do the high school coaching anymore, I do the summer program. And that's kind of what I do. I do some Tiger fantasy camps and those things, and get to see some of those folks, and then went over and played the Yankees and saw some of the guys there, when I played for the Yankees a little bit. So right now, I'm freezing my ass off in Kentucky, but other than that, that's it. Working for Pepsi Cola, coaching baseball, and trying to get my golf down to scratch - I'm getting closer, but don't get to play all year round. That's it - trying to be a good grandpa, how's that?

MIKE TORREZ: I still have my MAT Premiums International Inc. [matpremiums.com] business in New York. I put company logos on t-shirts, coffee mugs, hats. I'm going on 23 years with the company. It's an ASI company - Advertising Specialty Inc. - where you put logos on jackets, golf balls. And I target corporations and talk to them. They all buy giveaways, and that's what I sell them - put their logos on anything and everything and give them away.

BOBBY VALENTINE: I am doing a million things - my life is full of joy and challenges. I own restaurants, I have a film company, and I'm the executive director of athletics at a Division I School with 32 Division I teams with 800 athletes, I run a youth sports academy and national tournament play business. I'm doing a lot of things.

STEVE ZABRISKIE: I am blessed to be doing what I love to do, and that is I'm a part of the executive management in financial services for New York Life, which is the largest, oldest financial services firm in the country. I am in a position to help other people be successful, so to give back by helping to train and develop younger people in a career. Not that I know everything - I'm old, I've been around, I've learned a lot about what not to do. And I've been blessed to have multiple careers, and I've had success, and I don't regret any of that stuff. Are there things that I would go back and do differently? Absolutely. We've all made mistakes and I've made more than most. But I'm in a position now where I can really help other people and I'm with a company and a job in that company that enables me to do that, and that jazzes me, and that's why I still get out of bed every morning - thankfully, I'm blessed that I don't have to.

So I'm doing exactly what it is I want to be doing, I'm blessed to be doing it in a part of the country that is home to me and is one of the most beautiful places - even though I don't drink wine, I'm in wine country! And the weather is awesome, the scenery is beautiful, and the people are great. And I love the people I work with. I'm going to keep doing it as long as I can physically do it. I've had some health challenges - major ones, lately - but nothing that hasn't been overcome. So I'm blessed to keep putting one foot in front of the other, and it's fun for me, and it's very rewarding. And I still get paid, too - so that's a bonus! It's a great company and a great industry to be in. I'm happy.

PAT ZACHRY: Retired from being a schoolteacher a few years ago. My wife retired this past year, also - she was an educator. She was a teacher as a principal, for about the last 15 years. Everything is great - we're just raising grandchildren and trying to play as much golf as I can when the weather allows down here [Waco, Texas]. Everything is going pretty good.

OTHER BOOKS BY GREG PRATO

SPORTS:

Sack Exchange: The Definitive Oral History of the 1980s New York Jets

Dynasty: The Oral History of the New York Islanders, 1972-1984

Just Out of Reach: The 1980s New York Yankees

MUSIC:

A Devil on One Shoulder and an Angel on the Other: The Story of Shannon Hoon and Blind Melon

Touched by Magic: The Tommy Bolin Story

Grunge is Dead: The Oral History of Seattle Rock Music

No Schlock....Just Rock! [A Journalistic Journey: 2003-2008]

MTV Ruled the World: The Early Years of Music Video

The Eric Carr Story

Too High to Die: Meet the Meat Puppets

The Faith No More & Mr. Bungle Companion

Overlooked/Underappreciated: 354 Recordings That Demand Your Attention

Over the Electric Grapevine: Insight into Primus and the World of Les Claypool

Punk! Hardcore! Reggae! PMA! Bad Brains!

Iron Maiden: '80 '81

Survival of the Fittest: Heavy Metal in the 1990's

Made in the USA
Columbia, SC
13 November 2018